Curtains, Draperies & Shades

By the Editors of Sunset Books and Sunset Magazine

Lane Publishing Co.,
Menlo Park, California

A book of ideas as well as how to's...

Whether you're shopping for ideas or looking for how-to information—or both —this book will guide you in planning and making your window treatments.

The color photographs in the first chapter illustrate the versatility of curtains, draperies, and decorative shades...and ways they can be effectively combined. The photographs also show the role fabric, pattern, and color play in a decorating scheme.

Our second chapter contains directions for making different curtain, drapery, and shade styles. Each style has step-by-step instructions (presented so that even a novice at sewing can follow them) that adapt to suit the measurements of your window.

Putting together a book like this calls for teamwork and input from different sources. In addition to the many designers whose names appear with the photo captions, we are grateful to the following places for their assistance: The Cotton Works, Customhouse Draperies, Pierre Deux, Los Gatos Porch, and Poppy Fabric.

In particular, we wish to thank Dorothy Perry, our professional consultant, and Susan Watkins, who so generously shared with us their time, knowledge, and expertise.

Staff Editors:

Diane Petrica Tapscott
Susan Warton
Christine Barnes
Linda J. Selden

Design: Cynthia Hanson

Photography: Steve W. Marley

Illustrations: Mary Knowles

Editor, Sunset Books: Elizabeth L. Hogan

Eleventh printing March 1989

Contents

Black and buff gingham
pinch-pleated tieback draperies
with matching wallpaper
compose a casual country
setting for treasured antiques.
Design: Diane Lacey-Baker.

DECORATING IDEAS
for Your Windows

Good design—how does it happen? You can't actually break down the process into definite steps because the design for a good window treatment evolves through consideration of your window and your room, plus all the decorative elements of style, fabric, color, texture, and pattern. To design your own window treatments, first throw all the "rules" out the window and make room in your mind for unlimited imaginative variations on curtains, draperies, and decorative shades.

You probably already have something in mind for your windows, perhaps have seen a treatment you like. Before you commit yourself to a specific idea, raise a few questions of function: Do you need a treatment like a hard-working shade for privacy and light control, or stationary curtains or draperies to frame an outstanding view? Even if privacy and light control aren't critical, you may still want to install an energy-conserving window covering.

What about the window's design and the rest of the room? Do you want to camouflage a nondescript frame surrounding a double-hung window or highlight unusual architectural detail in a bay? A special window style section on pages 8–9 will guide

Lilting print of this bordered Roman shade brings out a window set between cupboards, adds cool color to warm wood and natural tones. Design: Corinne Wiley.

you in choosing appropriate treatments for typical and problem windows. Whatever the window style, you'll want the treatment to complement the room's furniture, floors, walls, and accessories.

With these preliminary considerations in mind, decide which of the three basic treatments—curtains, draperies, or decorative

shades—will work best for you.

Say "curtains" and most people think "kitchen"—but curtains adapt beautifully for every room. Perky and simple to make, a curtain attaches to the rod by hooks, rings, or fabric tabs, or has a rod pocket for the rod to slip through; generally, curtains are stationary—if they do open and close, it's done by hand. Café curtain panels cover part of the window (multiple tiers may cover the whole window), usually for a casual effect; full-length curtains, which go from the window top to the sill or beyond, can have a surprisingly sophisticated appearance.

The heavier, more elegant fabrics often used for draperies give these window treatments their luxurious flow and excellent insulating qualities. Always pleated, a drapery is fastened over a rod by rings or hooks; it may traverse or hang as a stationary panel.

Versatility is the shade's great virtue. Both functional and decorative, shades roll or pull up and down for efficient, convenient light control. They come in an array of styles—from crisply tailored to softly poufed—to fit almost every decorating concept.

Once you've chosen the treatment style, turn your attention to the materials you'll need and to the project directions. A fabrics

Simple curtains can be fancy, too.
Full-length rod-pocket curtains
with headings on fabric-covered rod
break gracefully at the floor, flank-
ing, rather than covering, glass
doors. Lush fabric is rayon and
acetate. Design: Leslie Batchelor.

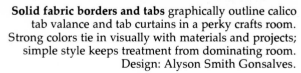

Solid fabric borders and tabs graphically outline calico
tab valance and tab curtains in a perky crafts room.
Strong colors tie in visually with materials and projects;
simple style keeps treatment from dominating room.
Design: Alyson Smith Gonsalves.

A sense of harmony, a touch of elegance result
from matching a tablecloth to a wide window of
full-length, multiple-shirred curtains.
Design: Diane Tapscott.

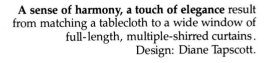

Curtains give you choices...there's a style for every mood, from romantic ruffles to crisply tailored pleats.

Crisp white café curtains, pleated and scalloped, unify a bay window and walls, create a simple backdrop for colorful room accents. Design: Joan Thompson.

Rain or shine, the mood's always sunny. Gently ruffled tieback curtains with valance on top and cafés underneath help turn a corner window into a cheerful, cozy place. Design: Alyson Smith Gonsalves.

Elegant and traditional, draperies lend a quiet note of formality to the windows they wrap.

Decorative one-way traverse rods make it possible to pull both panels of these pinch-pleated draperies on rings out from the corner, exposing all of the glass. Design: Ruth Soforenko.

Floor-to-ceiling stationary draperies with box pleats lengthen a blocky double-hung window. Narrow cornice repeats the border print on mock shade and drapery edges; fabric-covered cords tie draperies back. Design: Lois Lugonja.

The most traditional treatment can also be the most versatile. Pinch-pleated draperies of sheer linen, hung from a header, break up a floor-to-roof glass area without destroying the visual flow from indoors to outdoors. Design: Elva Powell.

Appareled like the spring, different windows wear the same fresh floral draperies, traditionally pinch-pleated and tied back. White roller shades with green accents reverse the scheme of rich green walls with white trim. Design: Corinne Wiley.

Peach and blue trim accentuates the classic design of pinch-pleated satin tieback draperies. Sheer draperies underneath open and close for privacy and light control. Design: Rita Williams, John Rossetti.

**Fabric patterns, echoed in wallpaper, tablecloths,
perhaps a throw of cushions,
can unify and brighten interiors.**

Flexible, efficient Roman shades in a bright bay window start out low in the morning when the sun pours
in, are easily raised as the day wears on. A square of matching fabric on a round table unifies shapes and patterns
into a decorative whole. Design: Corinne Wiley.

Low tiebacks keep stationary pinch-pleated draperies from fluttering in the breeze when casement window is open. Unity of fabric and wallpaper integrates the small window into the total room. Design: Leslie Batchelor.

Ruffled gingham curtains with valance define a recessed dormer window; matching ruffled accessories draw the eye into the room, uniting window with furnishings. Design: Diane Lacey-Baker.

Calico colors in pinch-pleated tieback draperies on rings match wallpaper, enlivening corner kitchen windows. Design: Pam Farnsworth.

White is the common element that unites romantic ruffled curtains with valance, striped and scalloped roller shade, and floral wallpaper. Design: John Rossetti.

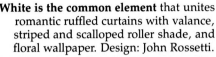

The basic motif and colors are similar—it's the bold disparity in scale that dramatically sets apart these stationary tieback curtains from the bordered Roman shades underneath. Design: Corinne Wiley.

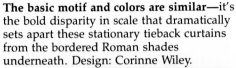

Mix patterns with audacity when colors in contrasting fabrics relate. Sprightly Roman shades set off vibrant rod-pocket curtain panels on a fabric-covered rod; matching window seat cushions complete the treatment. Design: Diane Tapscott.

Windows and walls can be daringly different—and still work—when one overall pattern echoes part of another in color or design. Roman shades in a bay window pick up elements in bold wallpaper. Small tassels decorate gently scalloped edges of valances and shades. Design: Sharon Bishop.

A medley of contrasting yet related patterns creates a fresh, lively atmosphere.

Multiple patterns...one mood. Keeping everything in the same spirit is the secret of a successful mix. Heading on rod-pocket curtains is separated and fluffed out for a pronounced three-dimensional effect. Design: Martha Baum and Sharon Marston.

Pale and understated tones are flexible to work with, pleasant to live with.

Floor-to-ceiling rod-pocket curtains with headings on fabric-covered rod frame French doors. Design: Diane Van Voorhis.

Neutral windows, neutral walls blend to create a state of inviting tranquillity. Full-length rod-pocket curtains of heavy cotton get their deep folds and soft heading from tight shirring on a decorative rod. Sash curtain admits light but gives some privacy.
Design: Diane Van Voorhis.

Lined to the edge in a solid fabric, these printed pinch-pleated draperies are folded and tied back for the perfect built-in edge emphasis. Decorative white rings and rod punctuate top of draperies.
Design: Pam Farnsworth.

When the view outside deserves to be seen, try an elegant treatment such as this gossamer Roman shade. Tapes stitched vertically to the front add design detail, hide rings and cords attached on back.

Fine design in these bordered Roman shades complements the rich architectural features of a Tudor-style bay. Design: Corinne Wiley.

Quietly framing a snug window seat hideaway, oyster white draperies under a cornice emphasize the definite horizontal and vertical lines in walls and ceiling. Design: Michael Taylor.

The challenge of a special window is to dress it up without overpowering its unique look and shape. Sash curtains cover the lower portion of arched windows; fabric fans on top are stretched on custom-bent rods and gracefully tied like chignons. Design: Patricia Wesley.

**Whether bay, arched, or
paned in leaded glass, noteworthy windows
deserve noteworthy dressings.**

Ideal treatment for a distinctive window, this Roman shade covers a little or a lot of the window, but still shows off the handsome window casing. Design: Corinne Wiley.

**A kitchen bouquet...
pick a pretty style
that graces the window
while inspiring the cook.**

Tucked into window frames, scalloped café curtains on fabric-covered rods show off window casings and multiple panes. An oval tension rod holds each curtain snugly in place; clip-on oval rings simplify installation and removal for cleaning. Design: Christine Barnes.

Reminiscent of a country kitchen, rod-pocket curtains tied with thick, fabric-covered cords add to the rustic charm of walls, floor, and furniture. Fabric-covered rod continues the casual mood. Design: Nancy Bostwick.

Simple-to-make tieback rod-pocket curtains with headings grace a kitchen window, blend with boldly patterned walls. Design: Ginny Zalesky.

Trio of eyelet-trimmed hourglass curtains adorns door and windows in an old-fashioned kitchen. Made with outside edges slightly longer, hourglass curtains are pulled in and banded at the center for a taut effect. Flat sash rods allow curtains to lie close to windows. Design: Alyson Smith Gonsalves.

Bedroom windows are beautifully treated with problem-solving in mind, bestowing privacy and light control.

The perfect place for a cat nap, a recessed window overlooking a bay gets treated to pinch-pleated canvas stationary draperies, tied back at the window, left full over side walls. To help the stitched Roman shade fold up, narrow wooden dowels are slipped through wide horizontal tucks. Design: Corinne Wiley.

It takes only one twin sheet to make this fresh one-way tieback curtain. Decorative band of the sheet becomes the wide tie; fabric strips sewn to curtain top are tied into bows over a brass curtain rod. Design: Alyson Smith Gonsalves.

Stunning bow window wears luxuriant stationary pinch-pleated draperies on a curved drapery rod; complementary roller shades in sophisticated white and Wedgwood blue give the final touch. Design: Jean Chappell.

Red, white, and dainty, this triple treatment combines full-length rod-pocket tieback curtains, café curtains, and a simple roller shade. Design: Sharon Bishop.

**The bathroom may
be small, but its latitude
for window creativity
is wide and wonderful.**

**Harmony—in fabric, wallpaper,
and accessories**—makes the room
seem larger. Full-length rod-pocket
curtains shirred on a wood pole
are tied high to show more
window; matching fabric roller
shade provides privacy. Design:
Jean Chappell.

Sash curtains on adjustable tension rods cover just enough of these bathroom windows to give privacy while they frame the serene waterfront world beyond. Design: Alyson Smith Gonsalves.

Poufed balloon shade matches wallpaper for a gift-wrapped look in a very small space; sash curtain on tension rods contributes the delicate finishing touch. Design: Esther H. Reilly.

Treat window and wall in related print fabrics and paper for a subdued, harmonious effect. Reverse-roll roller shade goes under rod-pocket tieback curtains with heading. Design: Ruth Soforenko.

The ideas start here, amid bolts and bolts of fabrics in an inspiring—and sometimes overwhelming—assortment of fibers, colors, and patterns.

How to Make
CURTAINS, DRAPERIES & SHADES

Transforming yards of alluring fabric into graceful folds of color and texture to enhance your windows and at the same time control privacy and light can be a highly satisfying creative experience. Even a simple roller shade can be a vivid personal expression in your home.

If you do your own custom design, you not only free yourself to use fabrics and styles that exactly reflect your taste—you also save a considerable amount of money. That saving may allow you to choose costlier fabrics or to extend your decorating adventure further than you had originally planned.

And making curtains, decorative shades—even floor-length draperies—is not as difficult as you may think. All you really need is care, patience, basic sewing skills, and plenty of time.

In this chapter, you'll find a wide variety of window decorating projects to choose from. Each has a corresponding set of step-by-step instructions that adapt to suit the measurements of your windows.

The next few pages offer guidance and helpful tips on organizing a work space; tools you'll need; measuring your windows;

buying, preparing, and cutting fabric; and sewing the basic seams and hems used in window treatments.

A place to work

Whether you're draping a wall of windows or whipping up a single snappy shade, you'll undoubtedly have to handle much more fabric than goes into clothing construc-

tion, and you're going to need plenty of elbow room. Mapping out and organizing a special work area is well worth the time it takes and the living space it steals.

A sewing room, with a large table and special nooks and crannies for supplies, is the ideal place to work. Perhaps you could temporarily convert the den or guest room to this purpose. Having a separate room allows you to come and go as you please without having to set everything up, then stash it all away, each time you work on your project. Your fabric will be safer, too, from accidental rumpling or soiling.

You'll need a large, flat surface on which to measure, cut, and sew. If you intend to decorate a number of windows, it might be worth investing in a piece of plywood as a tabletop. Set on two table-height sawhorses or atop a protected table, a 4 by 8-foot sheet of plywood will give you ample work space. A hollow flush door also makes a thrifty tabletop. Many stock doors weigh less than a sheet of plywood.

If the kids are willing to lend it to you, their ping-pong table can offer scads of space. Or, if you're going to have to work in a busy part of the house anyway, the dining room table—if it's rectangular—might be a likely choice.

To make any work surface you choose more serviceable, consider covering it with padding as explained under "Padding a work surface" (see next page). Here you'll also find details on selecting plywood.

Tools of the trade

After you have blocked out an area to work in, you'll need to gather a few supplies—some of which you may already own. The following list includes all the necessary tools for making window treatments, as well as some that are very useful though not absolutely essential.

Cutting tools

Bent-handled shears. Easier on the hands than regular scissor handles, the bent handle offers another advantage—allowing fabric to lie flat while you cut. Choose a pair that is 8 or 9 inches long; they're lightweight and the blades cut quickly. Cherish your shears— use them only on fabric (paper will dull the blades in short order).

Pinking shears. Available with saw-toothed or scalloped blades, pinking shears are useful for finishing seam edges so that they resist raveling.

Serrated shears. These 8-inch specialty shears are extremely sharp. Professionals use them on polyester fabrics, which have a tendency to dull ordinary blades.

Embroidery scissors. About 4 inches long, embroidery scissors are handy for clipping threads while sewing.

Thread clips. Even more convenient to use than embroidery scissors, this simple little tool snips threads in a snap.

Ironing tools

Iron. A steam iron is the most versatile, because it adjusts conveniently to a wide variety of fabrics.

Hand steamer. This tool is perfect for steaming out wrinkles and for giving a fresh look to window coverings after they are hung. It can also be used on hard-to-reach places, such as valances or cornices that are attached to boards. You can buy one where small appliances are sold.

Ironing board. Consider padding a large table to take the place of the ironing board, especially if you will be pressing quantities of fabric (see "Padding a work surface," next page). If you opt for the conventional ironing board, legs that adjust to different heights are an asset. A lower position allows you to sit comfortably as you iron.

Plastic spray bottle. Keep one handy near the ironing surface for extra moisture. But be careful: some bottles squirt too freely and may waterspot the fabric, particularly if it has a finish. Test a sample swatch first.

Press cloth. A 9 by 24-inch strip of unfinished muslin, cotton marquisette, or cheesecloth laid between iron and fabric protects the fabric from scorching and iron shine. It is especially recommended for the final pressing of seams and hems.

Measuring tools

Tape measures. A spring-return 12-foot steel tape measure assures easy, accurate measuring of windows and fabric. For measuring fabric, a 60-inch synthetic or fiberglass tape is convenient, but it is not designed to measure windows. Avoid cloth tapes—they tend to stretch.

Notebook. Record all measurements in a notebook so you can double-check them and refer to them easily later. You will need this notebook when you shop for fabric and also when you are ready to cut the yardage.

Carpenter's square. This tool is essential for squaring off the ends of yardage. You can buy a square at a hardware store. Watch for slight roughness on the edges that might snag fabric, particularly synthetics.

Yardstick. A metal or wood yardstick is useful for marking long cutting lines. Again, make certain the surface is perfectly smooth, so it doesn't snag the fabric.

Chalk pencil. In the notions section of fabric and department stores, you can find several kinds of chalk or wax pencils for marking fabric. Experiment on a sample swatch first. Some leave permanent marks after pressing.

Hem gauge. This 6-inch ruler with adjustable slide aids in measuring seam allowances and hems.

Sewing tools

Masking tape. Strips of it, laid down on the throat plate of your sewing machine, serve as handy guides for keeping seams and hems straight; see "A tape trick," page 48.

Needles. Use sewing machine needles that are compatible with the weight of your fabric. Check the needle package and your sewing machine manual for guidance. To machine-tack pleats, be sure to use a sturdy needle—size 16 or 18—for it may have to penetrate as many as 18 layers of fabric.

A packet of hand-sewing needles in assorted sizes should take care of most hand-sewing jobs. But tacking pleats by hand will require a special heavy-duty needle. For this job, buy a packet of repair needles.

Pins. Fine, sharp dressmaker pins, about 1¼ inches long, made from steel or stainless steel, are best but sometimes hard to find. Check upholstery suppliers in your area.

Stronger than dressmaker pins are T-pins, useful for holding plush or open-weave fabrics, which tend to swallow pins with tiny heads. If you make curtains with multiple-shirred headings (see page 70), you will need T-pins to secure the fabric to a padded surface while you work.

Keep safety pins on hand for pulling cords and tape through casings.

Padding a work surface

To ease many of the steps in making window coverings, you might want to cover your work surface with padding the way professionals do.

The method you choose for padding your work surface depends on whether you use a table or improvise with a sheet of plywood or a flush door.

Padding a table

Because steam from ironing can penetrate and damage the finish, you'll want to stay on the safe side and not pad a valuable wooden table. A table with a plastic laminate top or an off-season picnic table would be a better candidate for covering.

Here's all you need: two or three blankets or smooth coverlets (or use cotton batting—*not* polyester); an unpatterned sheet or enough canvas (available in 60 and 72-inch widths) to overlap the table by about 6 inches on all sides; 8 to 12 large safety pins; masking tape; and, if possible, a friend to help you—four hands are better than two.

1. Drape blankets over tabletop, making enough layers to provide at least ½-inch thickness (you can double blankets if, doubled, they are still large enough to cover table and drape over sides).

2. Smooth the blankets. Then, starting at one end, fasten corners tightly on underside of table with safety pins. Move to opposite end, then pull blankets as taut as you can and fasten remaining corners (see illustration A).

3. Secure dangling blanket edges to underside with masking tape.

4. Cover blanketed tabletop with sheet or canvas; smooth and fasten as you did blankets. With a canvas covering, you can accomplish an even tighter fit by dampening the entire surface with water from a spray bottle. As the canvas dries, it will shrink tightly over the padding.

Padding a plywood sheet or a door

To improvise a work surface, you can choose either a sheet of plywood or a hollow flush door—the latter will be lighter in weight, but also smaller. As a base for either one, you can use a table (protect the top by laying a blanket over it first) or a pair of sawhorses. If you choose sawhorses, you'll need plywood that is rigid—¾ to 1 inch thick. Plywood supported by a table can be ½ inch thick.

Here's all you need: a 4 by 8-foot sheet of ½ to 1-inch-thick plywood or a door of similar size; a staple gun; 2 or 3 blankets or smooth coverlets (or use cotton batting—*not* polyester); an unpatterned sheet or 3 yards of 60-inch-wide canvas; and someone to help you, if possible—this job goes much faster with two people working.

1. Lay blankets on floor, making enough layers to provide at least ½-inch thickness (you can double blankets if, doubled, they are still large enough to cover and fold around wood). Center plywood or door on top.

2. Starting at middle of one long side, fold blankets over edge and secure with 4 staples, placed about 2 inches apart (see illustration B).

3. Move around to opposite side and, pulling blankets as taut as possible, secure with staples as in step 2.

4. Repeat steps 2 and 3 on remaining sides.

5. Go back to starting point. Then continue stapling blanket in 12-inch segments (staples 2 inches apart) on both sides of center, constantly pulling blankets taut.

6. Repeat step 5 on all sides until you've worked all the way out to corners.

7. Staple corners as shown in illustration C.

8. Lay canvas or sheet flat on floor; center blanketed wood on top. Fasten as you did blankets. If using canvas, dampen entire surface with water from a spray bottle; as canvas dries, it will shrink tightly over padding.

Illustration A

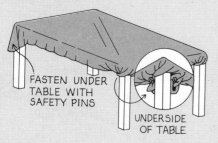

FASTEN UNDER TABLE WITH SAFETY PINS

UNDERSIDE OF TABLE

Illustration B

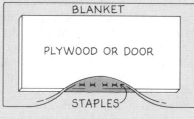

BLANKET

PLYWOOD OR DOOR

STAPLES

Illustration C

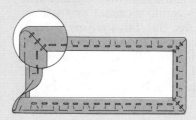

Window Arithmetic

The projects in this book are designed to adapt to the dimensions of your windows. So after you select a style of window treatment, the first step in turning your dream into reality is measuring portions of your window (or windows). Measuring is critical—amazing as it may seem, a miscalculation of even an inch or two could leave you short yards of fabric.

Using a steel tape, measure each window—even if they appear to be identical. Double-check each measurement, and be sure to write each down in your notebook for future reference.

Start with hardware

Before measuring for fabric, you must know where the curtain or drapery rod—or shade hardware—will be placed on your window.

In the project sections, pages 51–103, you'll find specific information on hardware for each style, as well as suggestions for its placement. The exact position is up to you—it will depend on the type of window you have and how much of the wall or frame you want to cover with fabric.

If you want your curtains or draperies to open wide enough to expose the entire glass area, read "Allowing for stackback" (next page).

Choose and purchase any new hardware before you start measuring, because its dimensions will affect your calculations. Install it at this point, too, if you can; seeing the hardware in place will help you to visualize finished results. But if this means dismantling an existing window covering and leaving the window exposed, you may decide to install the hardware later. If so, just make light pencil marks on the wall or frame to indicate the top of the rod (or roller or wooden board, in the case of a shade) and where the brackets will go.

Whether you install brackets at the outset or mark their positions with pencil, be sure that the rod (or roller or mounting board for a shade) will be perfectly level.

Measuring width and length

After hardware is either installed or its position marked with pencil, you have a starting point from which to measure the width and length of your curtain, drapery, or shade.

You make and record in your notebook two sets of measurements. The first set of measurements is the *finished width* and the *finished length*. These are the dimensions of the finished treatment as it will hang, closed, at the window. They do not include allowances for what is hidden from view—headings, hems, seams, fullness—nor do they allow for the extra fabric required to match patterns.

The second set of measurements is calculated from the finished width and length measurements.

These are the *total width*—from which you can work out how many fabric widths you will need—and the *cut length*.

Finished width

Measuring the finished width is a simple task, but it varies slightly depending on the style of window covering and hardware you've selected.

Curtains and draperies. To find the finished width for curtains and draperies, just measure the length of the rod with a steel tape measure. Then add measurements for returns and overlaps, if there are any. Two-panel pleated cur-

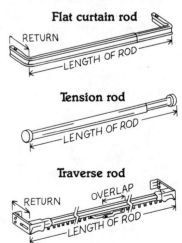

Flat curtain rod

RETURN — LENGTH OF ROD

Tension rod

LENGTH OF ROD

Traverse rod

RETURN — OVERLAP — LENGTH OF ROD

Allowing for stackback

Curtains and draperies that open to expose the entire glass area—or most of it—need room to stack beyond the glass. This area is called the "stackback."

For most fabrics you'll need to allow one-third the width of the glass area (or the area you wish to expose) for the stackback. If your fabric is unusually bulky, add to this allowance 1 extra inch for each width of fabric you're using.

The drawings below illustrate rod placements for two-way and one-way draw treatments.

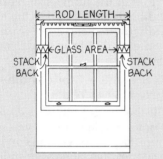

For a two-way draw treatment, *place half the stackback amount on each side of the glass.*

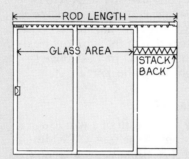

For a one-way draw treatment, *place entire stackback on one side of glass.*

tains (pages 59–62) that are hung from flat or café curtain rods look best if they overlap at the center. Since these rods don't have provision for overlap, you must add 3½ inches to the finished width measurement. Traverse rods have a built-in overlap, so the measurement is more obvious.

Shades. Whether you plan to mount a roller shade on the frame or between the jambs, finding its finished width is easy—merely measure the length of the visible wooden portion of the roller.

Roller

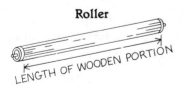

For a Roman, Austrian, and balloon style, the finished width depends on where you hang the wooden mounting board. If it is mounted outside the frame, the finished width is simply the width of the area you want to cover.

But if you plan to hang your shade between the window jambs, measuring the finished width takes a few extra steps. Because windows are often slightly out of square, you should measure the jamb-to-jamb width in three places: at the top of the glass, at the midpoint, and at the sill. To be sure of enough ease, subtract ¼ inch from the narrowest measurement, and use this figure as your finished width.

Finished length

To measure the finished length, you need to know exactly where the treatment will start and end. These boundaries are determined by the style of covering and hardware you've chosen and by your placement of the hardware.

Starting point. For curtains and draperies, you begin measuring the finished length at the top of the rod (or penciled rod position); for shades, at the top of the roller or board.

The starting point must be adjusted, in the case of curtains and draperies, to allow for headings, rings, or ceiling mountings. This adjustment is explained with the illustrations shown below and on the following page.

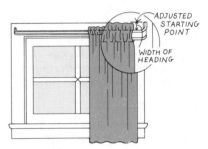

For gathered headings, *measure up from the top of the rod, a distance equal to the desired heading.*

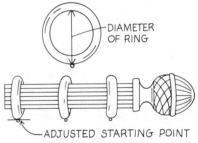

For curtains hung by rings, *the adjusted starting point is the bottom of the ring. (If hardware is not yet installed, measure from the point marked for the top of the rod to the sill, apron, or floor; then subtract the ring's diameter, as shown, to find the finished length.)*

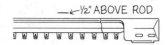

With wall or frame-mounted *traverse rods or for pleated curtain headings, measure from a point ½ inch above the rod.*

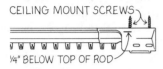

For ceiling-mounted *traverse treatments, measure from a point ¼ inch below top of rod.*

With decorative *traverse rods, measure from the bottom of the ring. (If hardware is not yet installed, measure as for curtain rings on previous page.)*

Carefully measure from the starting point—or the adjusted starting point—to the place where you want the curtain, drapery, or shade to end. This measurement —in inches—is the finished length.

Lower hems. Curtains, draperies, and shades are most pleasing to the eye when they appear to end in line with either the window or the floor. When the lower edge falls midway between, the effect is visually disturbing. As a rule, plan to end a treatment ¼ inch short of the window sill, exactly at the bottom of the apron, or ½ inch short of the floor. (Where there is a deep carpet, lay a piece of thin cardboard on the carpet to use as a base when you measure.) There are two exceptions—if you use an open-weave fabric or live in a particularly humid area, leave an inch between window treatment and floor. In double treat-

ments, the inner panel should be 1 inch shorter than the outer panel.

Certain situations call for special adjustments in length. Contemporary windows are often built without wooden frames or aprons. In designing a short treatment for such a window, position the lower edge 5 inches below the sill—then the back of the hem won't be visible from outside.

When furniture is built in below the window, the treatment usually looks better if it ends ½ inch short of the furniture, rather than at the sill or apron.

If you have any reason to believe that your heating source may pose a fire hazard, keep the lower edge of the window treatment at least 7 inches above it— or choose a short style.

Total width

The total width of a window covering is the finished width in inches (from your notebook), multiplied for fullness, plus allowances for side hems.

Finished Width × Fullness + Side Hem Allowances = Total Width

From this figure, you'll be able to determine the number of fabric widths needed in your project. Though seam allowances for curtains and draperies make up part of the actual total width, they do not use enough fabric to affect the number of fabric widths you'll need. Note: There is no flexibility in the width of a shade; therefore, you must also include seam allowances when calculating the total width. For more details on measuring for shades, see individual projects starting on page 87.

Fullness. Deep, luxurious folds are more appealing than scanty ones. For ample fullness in curtains and draperies, multiply the finished width by 2½ for medium and heavy fabrics. Sheer material needs even more— multiply the finished width by 3. See individual projects for exceptions.

Side hems. Unless otherwise specified in a project, side hems are doubled, 1½ inches wide —which means you add a 3-inch allowance

for each doubled side hem in the treatment.

How many fabric widths? Fabric off the bolt is typically 45, 48, or 54 inches wide, though it sometimes is possible to find fabrics as wide as 118 inches (these are sheer fabrics imported from Europe). Drapery lining, though, is generally 48 inches wide; if you are lining your treatment, and face fabric and lining are different widths, you will have to calculate the number of widths of lining fabric separately from those of face fabric.

To find the number of fabric widths required, divide the total width (in inches) of the covering by the width of the fabric you plan to use.

Total Width ÷ Fabric Width = Number of Widths

If the result from your division is not a whole number, you must round it off. For curtains and draperies, we suggest rounding off to the larger whole number if the fractional part is greater than ½ (for instance, 3.7 widths rounds off to 4) or rounding off to the smaller whole number if the fractional part is less than ½ (3.2 rounds off to 3). The fabric width lost this way does not significantly reduce the fullness.

For shades, you must always round off to the next full width of fabric.

Most curtains and draperies open at the center; each half of the treatment is called a "panel." When you will have two panels in your finished treatment, you must divide the total number of fabric widths in half to determine how many widths and partial widths of fabric will make up each one. If this sounds confusing, it might help to make a sketch; draw full fabric widths at the center of the treatment and a partial width at each side. See also "Joining fabric widths," page 49.

How to figure total yardage for unpatterned fabric

Follow the steps below to calculate how much yardage you will need if you plan to use solid-color, unpatterned fabric. With many of today's faintly flecked fabrics, it is a matter of guesswork to decide whether or not a fabric is unpatterned. For practical purposes, consider the fabric solid-color if there is no discernible variation in color or texture when you stand several feet away from it.

One other tip—along with your invaluable notebook for recording measurements, a pocket calculator is a great boon. Double-check your math to avoid errors.

Though completion of step 5 below will give you the total yardage required for your treatment, we suggest that you buy an extra ½ yard for sample pressing and stitching.

1. Finished width × fullness + side hem allowances = **Total width** (for shades, also include seam allowance)
2. Total width ÷ fabric width = **Number of fabric widths** (round off if necessary)
3. Finished length + bottom hem allowance + heading allowance + 1 inch = **Cut length**
4. Number of fabric widths × cut length = **Total length in inches**
5. Total length in inches ÷ 36 = **Total yardage**

Cut length

To find the cut length, add to the finished length figure allowances for bottom hem and heading, plus 1 inch to allow for raveling and squaring the ends.

Finished Length + Bottom Hem Allowance + Heading Allowance + 1 Inch = Cut Length

Total yardage for unpatterned fabric

Calculating the total yardage for unpatterned fabrics is simple if you know the number of fabric widths required and the cut length. (Patterned fabrics require special calculations, which are explained in the next column.)

First, multiply the number of fabric widths by the cut length to get the total length, in inches. Then divide the result by 36 to convert it from inches to the number of yards to buy.

Number of Fabric Widths × Cut Length = Total Length in Inches; Total Length in Inches ÷ 36 = Total Yardage

Adjustments for patterned fabric

You'll probably have to buy extra yardage if you plan to use a fabric with a printed design or a woven one (piqué, for example); with few exceptions, the "repeats" in the pattern must be matched when you make your window treatment.

To calculate yardage for patterned fabric, first follow the directions for unpatterned fabrics (starting this page) to determine the total width and cut length measurements. The total width will be the same as it would

for unpatterned fabric—but the cut length figure will have to be adjusted.

Must patterns match?

Such a tiny pattern repeat as the dot on dotted Swiss might not need to be matched for gathered styles, such as rod-pocket café curtains. But don't let the size of the repeat fool you. Even the smallest patterns can look mismatched after fabric has been pleated for a curtain or drapery or seamed for a shade. For these styles, always match the repeats.

Here's how you can check to see if the small repeats will need matching. While you're in the store, unroll enough yardage so that you can lay two sections of the patterned fabric side by side, with selvages aligned. Matching motifs in the pattern, arrange the fabric sections to make the pattern continue across the two widths as if they were one piece of fabric. Now shift one section of the fabric slightly—if you can't see any difference in the pattern, you can calculate total yardage according to the preceding directions for unpatterned fabrics. But if the pattern fluctuates jarringly, base your calculations on the size of the pattern repeat as explained further along.

Pattern placement

Before calculating for yardage, you should decide where you want the pattern repeats to fall on the finished treatment. Repeats on each width of fabric must match those on adjoining widths; also, repeats on each panel must match, and all the windows in the room should match.

Professionals follow a rule of thumb to decide where pattern repeats should fall. For floor-length panels, they place a full repeat just below the heading— the eye travels here first. Because the bottom is the focal point of apron and sill-length treatments, the placement is just the reverse —a full repeat ends at the hem.

Full repeat below heading

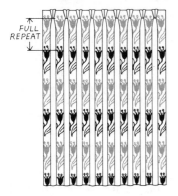

Full repeat at lower hem

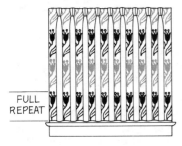

When both floor and sill or apron-length coverings hang in the same room, the rule for floor-length placement takes precedence— position full repeats just below the headings.

Measuring the repeat

To calculate extra yardage for matching patterns, you must measure (and record in your notebook) the height of the pattern repeat. If there is more than one

How to figure total yardage for patterned fabric

If the fabric you will use for your window treatment has a pattern, follow the steps below to calculate how much yardage you will need. If you are unsure whether or not your fabric is patterned—there are many borderline cases —read "Must patterns match?" on page 39 for guidance.

Besides your notebook for recording measurements, equip yourself with a pocket calculator if you possibly can. Double-check your math.

Note that even though you will have determined your total yardage by the time you complete step 6, you will actually have to buy a bit more. See "Those few crucial inches" on the next page. Besides the inches, we suggest an extra 1/2 yard for sample pressing and stitching.
1. Finished width × fullness + side hems
= **Total width** (for shades, also include seam allowance)
2. Total width ÷ fabric width (or usable fabric width)
= **Number of fabric widths** (round off if necessary)
3. Cut length ÷ repeat height = **Number of repeats needed for each cut length** (round off to next higher number)
4. Number of repeats needed for each cut length × repeat height
= **Adjusted cut length**
5. Adjusted cut length × number of fabric widths (Step 2)
= **Total length in inches**
6. Total length in inches ÷ 36 = **Total yardage**

set of repeats, measure the largest only.

Find the repeat height by measuring lengthwise from one motif within the repeat (a pink rose in a multicolored bouquet, for example) to the next identical motif (the next pink rose). Sometimes the repeat height is printed on the

selvage, but rather than rely on the figure given, measure the height yourself. Ask an experienced salesperson for help if you are at all unsure.

Matching widths is rarely a problem because most patterned fabric is designed to match at the selvages. However, occasionally it

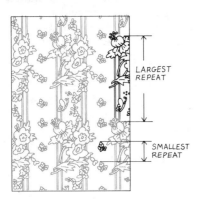

Repeat matches near selvages

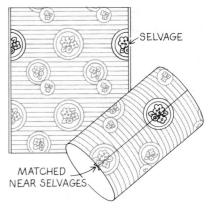

doesn't, which means that some of the actual fabric width must be sacrificed in order to match repeats at seams.

If the fabric does not match at the selvages, find the full repeat that falls closest to the selvage on each side. Measure from one motif (as near the center of one repeat as possible) across the width to its "twin" in the full repeat near the opposite selvage. Substitute this measurement—we'll call it usable width—for the actual fabric width when you calculate total yardage for patterned fabric that does not match selvage-to-selvage.

Repeat matches inside selvages

LOST FABRIC

USABLE WIDTH

Total yardage for patterned fabrics

Begin by determining the cut length measurement according to instructions for unpatterned fabrics (page 39), and record it in your notebook. Then, with measurements for cut length, repeat height, and (usable) fabric width in your notebook, you can calculate the total yardage for patterned fabrics.

First divide the cut length by the repeat height and round off to the next higher number if the result contains a fraction—this gives you the number of pattern repeats needed for each cut length. Then multiply this result by the repeat height to determine, in inches, the adjusted cut length. Next, multiply the adjusted cut length by the number of fabric widths to get the total length in inches. Finally, divide by 36 to convert this figure to yards.

Those few crucial inches

To make sure that pattern repeats will fall into the right position when your window covering is made up, it is crucial to start measuring total yardage at the right point in the pattern—rather than at the cut end of the yardage on its bolt. This means you may need to buy a little more fabric.

If you plan to have full repeats fall just below the headings (illustration A), find the first full repeat nearest the cut end. Measure from just above the repeat to the cut end to see if there is enough fabric for the heading allowance of the first cut length. If not, find the next repeat, deeper into the yardage, and measure again. If this provides the extra inches needed for heading allowance, measure total yardage from this point. Though this may mean buying ½ yard extra, it's essential if you want full repeats at the heading.

If you plan to have full repeats fall at the bottom (illustration B), unroll on the table a little more yardage than your adjusted cut length figure. Find the full repeat that would end just above the bottom hem.

Measure from the hemline repeat, deeper into the yardage, the distance allowed for the bottom hem. Then measure back from this point, toward the cut end, a distance equal to the adjusted cut length. From this point you can measure the total yardage.

Very infrequently, patterns are printed in a one-way direction that runs "backward," toward the center of the bolt. If this is the case with your fabric, simply reverse the preceding directions—follow those for hemline repeats if you want repeats to fall at the heading, and follow the directions for heading repeats if yours are to fall at the hem.

Where to start measuring total yardage for patterned fabric

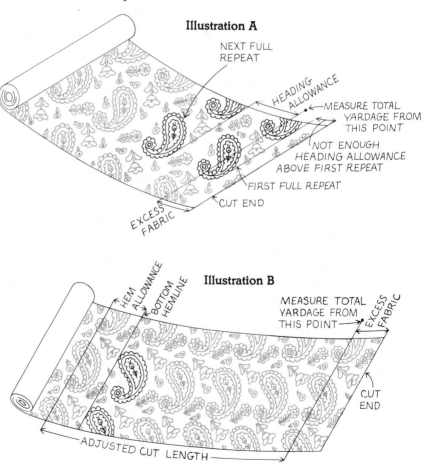

Illustration A

NEXT FULL REPEAT

HEADING ALLOWANCE

MEASURE TOTAL YARDAGE FROM THIS POINT

NOT ENOUGH HEADING ALLOWANCE ABOVE FIRST REPEAT

FIRST FULL REPEAT

CUT END

EXCESS FABRIC

Illustration B

HEM ALLOWANCE

BOTTOM HEMLINE

MEASURE TOTAL YARDAGE FROM THIS POINT

EXCESS FABRIC

CUT END

ADJUSTED CUT LENGTH

Selecting & Preparing Fabrics

Selecting fabric for window treatments can be frustrating as well as fun. Confronted with countless bolts of yardage in a kaleidoscope of colors, textures, and patterns, your senses are likely to overindulge to the point of pleasurable confusion. These pages will guide you in paring down the choices.

Once you've bought the fabric, you'll need to prepare it before sewing, in order to make sure the fabric will hang evenly and drape smoothly, with seams as inconspicuous as possible.

Fabrics, fibers & performance

Color, pattern, and texture are a fabric's most exciting characteristics, but when you're choosing materials for curtains, draperies, or shades, you'll want to know what fibers make up the fabric and whether or not the fabric will perform well in a given setting.

Will the fabric...?

Here are some questions to consider as you ponder the relative merits of myriad fabrics:

• *Will the fabric provide adequate insulation against temperature changes and sound?* Any fabric hung at the window and covering the glass area will act as an insulating buffer against noise and erratic temperature conditions. Why? Because the space between fabric and window— almost a "dead-air space"—prevents air currents (which carry heat, cold, and sound) from circulating. The degree of insulation will be determined by the type of fabric and style of covering you choose.

Heavy, tightly woven fabrics— antique satin or velvet, for instance—form a more compact barrier than a loosely constructed fabric. As for style, a pleated drapery with deep folds captures more air behind it than a flat roller shade does. And any lined treatment will be more insulative than any unlined one.

In addition, heavily textured fabrics are good choices for sound control, whether you want to block noise from the outside or keep the music from your stereo system from bouncing off the walls. These fabrics function in much the same way that acoustic ceilings do.

• *Will the fabric effectively block or cut back on light and glare?* The weave, weight, and color of a fabric determine how much light can pass through a window treatment. Lighter colors, sheer fabrics, and loose weaves pass the most light and are effective in reducing glare. On the other hand, tightly woven, heavy, dark fabrics eliminate most, if not all, light.

The style of your window treatment will also affect the amount of light that reaches your room. Draperies or curtains with many folds will hold back more light than treatments using less fabric —for instance, Roman shades.

Finally, there's the number of layers you incorporate into your treatment—the more layers, the less light. Layers that are movable give greater control over the amount of light entering the room.

• *Is the fabric stable, or will it shrink and stretch during climatic changes?* The particular construction of a window treatment fabric is also a factor in stability; loose weaves and yardage with heavy weft yarns have a greater tendency to sag, shrink, or ripple from temperature and humidity changes than closely woven fabrics with warp and weft yarns of equal weight.

• *Is the fabric durable and abrasion-resistant?* Some fabrics and fibers (especially synthetics) hold up better than others under repeated use and handling—a particularly important point if the material is intended for draw draperies or accompanying treatments underneath. There are special finishes that make fabrics resistant to soil, fungus, and insects—an important feature if the environment is warm and humid.

• *Will the fabric resist fading and sun rot?* The type of dye process used for a specific fabric determines how resistant it is to the damaging effects of light. Often the dye process is indicated on the selvage or on the bolt; if not, ask a salesperson.

For natural fibers, vat-dyeing produces the best results; for synthetics, solution dyeing is best. Surface-dyed or printed fabrics have the least resistance to fading; this is especially true of synthetics. It is best to incorporate a lining or protective sheer curtain into a window treatment that uses printed or surface-dyed fabrics.

Sun rot, on the other hand, is harder to control. No completely effective treatment or fiber type has yet been developed to resist the high temperatures to which window treatments are repeatedly subjected in direct and reflected sun situations. Mineral fibers (such as glass, which is not generally recommended for home sewing) come closest to being unaffected by the sun, with linen (a natural fiber) and a few of the synthetics—acrylics, polyesters, and acetate—having more resistance than other fiber types.

It's wise to line draperies or at least hang protective sheer curtains between them and the sun to cut back on exposure, especially in windows having western or southern exposures. In extreme sun conditions, consider incorporating blinds, shades, or aluminum-coated linings into your window treatment. The extra expense will save you money in the long run.

• *Is the fabric fire-resistant or flameproof?* Most fabrics sold for home decorating have been treated to prevent them from burning rapidly, if at all, should they be accidentally ignited. Wool, silk, and polyester are slow burners, but these and all other fibers should be, and usually are, treated with special finishes that retard flammability. To be certain, check the fiber content and care label on the bolt.

For details on buying lining fabrics, see "Lining," page 45.

To line or not to line?

The time and money it takes to add a lining are nothing if sun, seasonal temperature changes, noise, and a uniform appearance from outdoors are prime concerns.

Linings extend the life of window treatments by protecting the decorative face fabric from sun, abrasion, and, to some degree, air pollution.

Linings also improve the appearance of most curtains, draperies, and decorative shades by adding extra body. Some fabrics, though lovely, may become limp after hanging for a time—a lining gives such fabrics more fullness and keeps them looking fresh much longer. And lining a modestly priced fabric (sheets, for example) can make it look like a more costly decorator fabric.

Most lining fabrics for window treatments are made of cotton or rayon in a variety of weights. These linings are usually "sateen" fabrics—the name of a fabric made in a particular, tightly woven construction. You'll find sateen linings in white and off-white.

Some linings are aluminum-coated on the wrong side of the fabric. This coating reflects both heat and cold, giving the lining fabric even better insulative and protective qualities than uncoated linings.

For details on buying lining fabrics, see "Lining," page 45.

• *Can the fabric be easily cleaned?* Most drapery and curtain materials do best when dry-cleaned, for washing tends to remove special finishes and soften creases or folds; it can also shrink some fabrics.

Fiber facts

Fiber and fabric are two different things—the terms cannot be used interchangeably. Think of fiber—whether natural or synthetic—as a raw material from which cloth is eventually made; each fiber has certain specific characteristics. Fabric, on the other hand, is a material comprising a fiber or blend of fibers structured into a length of cloth with specific visual and textural characteristics. The idea behind blending fibers is to bring out the good qualities of each fiber, producing a superior fabric.

Since a given fiber's characteristics remain constant whether that fiber is used alone or in a blend, we offer the following information on the characteristics of fibers, rather than fabrics.

Acetate (synthetic)—Stable; sunfast when solution-dyed; drapes well; absorbent; will wrinkle; subject to abrasion; has insulating qualities; picks up static electricity; resists pollution, moths, mildew; melts rather than burns.

Acrylic (synthetic)—Stable and durable; colors stable but may darken slightly in sun; resists sun rotting; nonabsorbent; wrinkleproof; picks up static electricity; resists moths, mildew, abrasion; melts rather than burns.

Cotton (natural)—Stable and durable; fades in sun; will sun rot; will wrinkle and shrink during cleaning if not treated; nonstatic; resists moths and abrasion; can mildew; will burn unless treated.

Linen (natural)—Strong and durable; fades in sun; absorbent; will wrinkle unless blended with more stable fibers such as cotton or polyester (in humid climates, should be used in a blend with nonabsorbent synthetics such as nylon, acrylic, and polyester to prevent stretching and shrinking); nonstatic; resists moths and soil; will mildew; burns unless treated.

Modacrylic (synthetic)—Stable; sunfast; nonabsorbent; wrinkle-proof; subject to abrasion; has insulating qualities; picks up static electricity; resists pollution, moths, flame, mildew; non-allergenic. Blends of modacrylic and linen are not recommended for window treatments.

Nylon (synthetic)—Stable and durable; fades in sun; will sun rot; wrinkleproof; has insulating qualities; picks up static electricity; pills; resists abrasion, mildew, moths, soil; melts rather than burns.

Polyester (synthetic)—Stable and durable; sunfast; nonabsorbent; wrinkleproof; has insulating qualities; picks up static electricity; pills; resists abrasion, flame, mildew, moths, pollution.

Rayon (synthetic)—Nonstable unless treated; will sun rot unless lined; drapes well; will wrinkle unless blended with a more stable fiber; subject to abrasion; has insulating qualities; resists moths; will mildew; will burn unless treated.

Silk (natural)—Stable and durable; fades in sun; will sun rot; will wrinkle; picks up static electricity; resists abrasion and moths; will mildew; burns unless treated.

Triacetate (synthetic)—Stable if treated; sunfast; wrinkleproof; resists sun and pollution; burns unless treated.

Wool (natural)—Most stable if blended with synthetics; durable; fades in sun; will sun rot; reacts to humidity and temperature

changes; picks up static electricity; pills; resists abrasion; must be treated to resist moths and mildew; burns unless treated.

Shopping wisely

You'll probably find the best fabric selection, as well as the most knowledgeable salespeople, in stores that specialize in drapery and upholstery fabrics. But it makes good sense to allow plenty of time to shop in a variety of stores—department stores, decorator shops, and general fabric shops are all good possibilities. And while you're shopping, keep in mind the functional aspects of fabrics, as outlined on the preceding pages.

You will be making a sizable investment in money and time—and the fabric you choose is likely to hang in your home for years.

What to consider

Your first consideration while browsing among bolts of yardage undoubtedly will be appearance. If possible, take along paint chips and fabric swatches to compare colors, textures, and patterns with those of your walls and furnishings. Take a fabric sample home, as well. Some stores allow customers to borrow an entire bolt of fabric to see how it looks in a proposed setting.

If this isn't possible, buy a yard or so to try out at home. It's worth the cost, for a change in background color and lighting can alter the appearance of fabric—sometimes drastically. Also, you can test the fabric to see how smoothly it sews, or whether it wrinkles readily or waterspots.

It's wise to look over a large portion of the fabric. Unroll several yards, then gather one end in your hand. Does it drape well? Does the design or texture hold its own, without getting lost in the folds? Stand back several feet to see how it looks from a distance.

Check the fabric grain. To drape properly, the fabric you use must

have as straight a grain as possible—its crosswise threads running perpendicular to its lengthwise threads. Because it is virtually impossible to straighten the grain of the voluminous yardage required for most window treatments, and because many modern fabrics are treated in such a way that they can't be straightened no matter what the quantity, it is wise to buy fabric that is already straight.

If you can snip and pull a crosswise thread that spans the fabric width, close to its cut edge, this is the simplest way to check the grain. The pulled thread will meet at right angles with the selvages if the grain is straight. In many fabrics that have been treated with a special finish, you will not be able to pull a thread—in which case you must judge the straightness of the threads as best you can by eyesight.

Check the fabric, at the same time, to see how likely it is to stretch out of shape as you work with it. Often you can judge just by pressing or pulling it gently with your hand as the fabric lies on a flat surface.

Be very cautious when selecting a printed fabric. In nearly every case, the print will be slightly off-grain—veering at an angle from the lengthwise and crosswise threads. Often the misalignment is not severe enough to be noticeable. But if it is, you should choose a different fabric, for if the print is badly off-grain, the finished treatment will never hang properly and its seams will be likely to pucker.

To check patterned fabric, fold the fabric back a few inches, wrong sides together, aligning selvages. If the print runs evenly along the fold, it is fairly well aligned with the fabric grain. But if it wanders from one selvage to the other, the print is badly off-grain and the fabric should be put back on the shelf.

Checking the grain

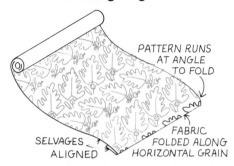

PATTERN RUNS AT ANGLE TO FOLD

SELVAGES ALIGNED

FABRIC FOLDED ALONG HORIZONTAL GRAIN

Off-grain printing is a matter of degree. If you feel uncertain about how much is too much, ask an experienced salesperson.

Lining. Choose a lining fabric that's compatible with the decorative fabric you've picked. Hold the two together to check whether or not they drape well as a pair. A delicate voile fabric would lose some of its character if you lined it with aluminum-coated lining, but a cotton sateen lining would be less obtrusive. For certain fabrics —open-weave casements, for example—you might even consider hanging a lining drapery or curtain on a separate rod so it doesn't spoil the airy look of the fabric. For more lining tips, see "To line or not to line?" on page 43.

Note that lining fabrics often come in narrower widths than decorative face fabrics. If you can find lining of the same width, it is a great help. If not, remember that you will have to make separate calculations for total yardage of lining.

Quality and practicality. Once you've narrowed your choices to several bolts of handsome fabric, it's time to face the hard facts of quality and practicality. For adequate insulation, will you need a tightly woven fabric? Will the airy open-weave you love provide the privacy you seek? Valuable information on fiber content is some-

times printed on the selvages, and special finishes to make fabrics sun or soil-resistant are listed on the label of the bolt. If you have further questions, talk with a reliable salesperson.

Cost. For most people, cost will be another important factor in choosing fabric. If you are on a tight budget, it's better to choose a less expensive fabric than to skimp on the amount of yardage. Luxuriously draped, such a fabric can look as elegant as one that costs more.

Buy from one bolt

When you've found a fabric that suits you perfectly, you should buy all you need at one time (plus an extra ½ yard for sample pressing and stitching, unless you bought a sample when you were selecting fabric). And if you possibly can, you should buy it all from one bolt. There are two reasons for this, one having to do with color, the other with pattern.

Usually the salesperson can estimate the amount of fabric on a bolt. If it's too little for your project, inquire about having a larger bolt special-ordered. That will probably take time, but it may be the very best solution.

Color. Because fabric bolts as a rule are not marked with dye lot numbers, there is no way of being certain that fabric from two different bolts was dyed at the same time in the same bath. Slight differences in color from one dye lot to another may be noticeable in the finished window treatment.

If you hope to avoid the delay that a special order would probably involve, try holding fabric from two bolts together, examining it in various kinds of light, looking for any perceptible differences. If you're unable to detect any difference at all, you would probably be safe to buy it. But even the slightest variation is likely to be intensified in the finished treatment.

Should you decide to buy from two bolts, we recommend that you not mix the fabrics at the same window. For example, if you have

three windows, buy enough from one bolt to make treatments for two of them; then from another bolt, buy all of the fabric for the third window, rather than making one panel from one bolt and one from another. To do this you'll need to think in terms of cut lengths, rather than total yardage, when the fabric is being measured. If you need four cut lengths and a bolt has enough fabric for three and a half cut lengths, that last half-length is useless to you and must not be counted in your total yardage. Finally, remember to mark the pieces clearly so you won't mix them during sewing.

Patterned fabric. If yours is a patterned fabric, follow all of the guidelines outlined under "Color" in the column at left. In addition, you will have to be certain that any yardage cut from a second bolt begins at the correct point in the pattern—determine this in exactly the same way you determined the starting point for measuring the first cut length. Most stores will not charge a customer for fabric that is wasted in this way because of a change of bolts, but you should discuss this in advance.

Again, the best and simplest way is to get a bolt that has adequate yardage for your entire project.

Flaws. As the salesperson counts off the yardage, inspect it carefully for flaws or inconsistencies in color or weave.

Choosing thread

The most commonly used threads are polyester and cotton-wrapped polyester; both come in size 40 (for heavy fabrics) and size 50 (for medium and lightweight fabrics). Both are available in great color variety.

Polyester thread is the best choice for most synthetic fabrics, though on tightly woven synthetics and blends it sometimes causes puckering. If the puckering problem occurs, try loosening the tension on your sewing machine, or try cotton-wrapped polyester thread instead.

Cotton-wrapped polyester thread is excellent for fabrics of natural fibers and natural fiber blends. Readily available, it combines the best qualities of polyester and mercerized cotton and is a particularly good thread for heavy fabrics, because it is very strong.

Avoid mercerized cotton thread for window treatments; it is susceptible to sun rot and fading, and it may shrink.

Colorless nylon monofilament thread—if you can find it—is ideal for blind-stitching hems. And because it is clear, sturdy, and not bulky, it can be used on all types and colors of fabric.

When matching thread to fabric, choose thread that is a slightly darker shade. For prints, match the thread to the predominant color. If you plan to zigzag stitch the seam edges of unlined treatments, match the thread for this finishing touch to the wrong side of the fabric (often different from the right side).

Should you preshrink?

Though many home sewers automatically preshrink new washable fabric, it is better not to do so when you make curtains, draperies, or shades. Many of today's fabrics are treated with finishes to make them wear well. If you preshrink them, some of the finish will wash away; besides losing its fresh, crisp appearance, the fabric will lose some of the properties the finish provides. For example, it may soil more easily.

As a rule, you should expect to dry clean window coverings rather than launder them. If you do anticipate laundering your window treatment, have the new fabric passed through a dry cleaner's steam roller. Steaming shrinks the fabric but is less likely to affect its

finish than laundering. (Steaming might also be a good precaution if the window treatment will be subjected to extreme humidity.)

Pressing professionally

Your iron will be your constant companion as you sew. Keeping the fabric wrinkle-free is well worth the hot and steamy time it takes—you'll be all the more assured of professional-looking results.

Pressing can save steps, too. For example, rather than folding and pinning a lengthy hem, it is speedier just to measure with a hem gauge, then fold and crease the hem in place with the iron. You will need fewer pins, and the fold will be neater.

Test a fabric swatch

Always test a sample of the fabric before you start pressing the new yardage. Now is the time to find out how much temperature, moisture, and pressure from the iron will produce smooth results without affecting the original character of the cloth; fabrics vary widely in this capacity. Some, like taffeta, may waterspot and should be pressed with a dry iron; others, like linen, need a tropical atmosphere to soothe away their wrinkles.

Safe ironing temperatures vary according to the fiber content of the fabric. If your fabric is a blend, let the most delicate fiber determine the heat level to use—for example, a 75 percent cotton, 25 percent polyester blend should be pressed at a medium-low setting.

It's safest to start testing with a low-temperature setting. Gradually increase the temperature until the fabric responds.

Ironing tips

Here are some pointers to keep in mind as you press your way through a project—from testing a sample swatch of fabric to touching up the last hem.

• **Keep iron surface clean** by scrubbing (when cool and unplugged!) with a nonabrasive scouring powder—a solution of baking soda and water works well.

• **A press cloth** helps to prevent scorching and iron shine. Use a strip of unfinished muslin, cotton marquisette, or cheesecloth; prewash it to remove sizing.

• **For fussy work**—pressing ruffles, for example—set the temperature slightly lower than normal for the fabric.

• **Protect heat-sensitive fabric** (any fabric that requires the "low" setting on the iron) by covering the ironing board with extra padding, such as flannel or another soft fabric.

• **Press the wrong side** of fabric to be safe. Never press the right side if the fabric is embossed (moiré), glazed (chintz), highly textured (damask), or embroidered. Press scalloped edges on the wrong side over thick padding.

Cutting lengths

After pressing the new yardage, you are ready to cut it into the lengths required for your project. You will need the cut length measurement (from your notebook); a large, flat work surface; a yardstick and carpenter's square; and a chalk pencil. Use one of the following methods, depending on whether or not your fabric is patterned.

Unpatterned fabric

Your first step in cutting lengths from fabric with no discernible pattern in its weave is to square off one cut end of the yardage. Lay the fabric, wrong side up, on a flat surface. Align one blade of the carpenter's square along one selvage of the fabric, close to one cut end, at a point where you'll be able to mark a line across the full width of the fabric. Using the other blade of the square as a straightedge, draw a chalkline across the width, perpendicular to the selvage; use a yardstick to extend the line to the opposite selvage. With the carpenter's square, check that the line meets the opposite selvage in a perfect right angle. Cut along the chalkline.

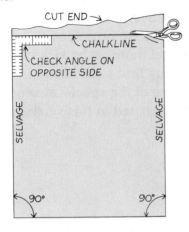

How to cut lengths. After squaring the first end, measure down *each* selvage a distance equal to the cut length; clip selvages at this point. Using a yardstick as a straightedge, draw a chalkline across the width of the fabric between the clips. After checking with a carpenter's square to be sure each corner is a true right angle, cut along the chalkline; this is the first squared-off length.

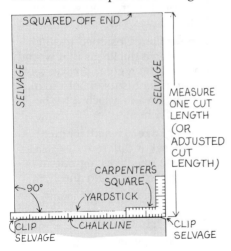

Continue to measure, mark, and cut, until all lengths are cut.

Patterned fabric

Virtually all prints and some woven pattern repeats run slightly off-grain. Though the misalignment is usually hard to see at close range, the pattern on the finished window covering might look oddly slanted if you were to follow the grain rather than the print when squaring off ends, cutting lengths, and sewing seams. Therefore, when you cut print fabric for window coverings, follow the lines of the pattern rather than the grain of the fabric.

Squaring off patterned fabric

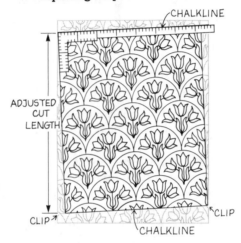

Note: *This illustration is exaggerated to clarify our point. If pattern is this off-grain, the fabric should not be used.*

Because the pattern will be your guide, you may have to square off each length along the sides as well as at the ends, as explained further along.

Squaring off first end. On a flat surface, smoothly lay out enough yardage, right side up, to equal a little more than one adjusted cut length. If you like, tape it in place with masking tape, or pin it to the padding if you have padded your work surface.

Place one blade of the carpenter's square along a horizontal line of motifs at the point where you started measuring total yardage when you bought the fabric. Using a yardstick to extend the line, draw a chalkline across the fabric width. Cut along this line.

How to cut lengths. To cut the first squared-off length, follow instructions for "How to cut lengths" under "Unpatterned fabrics," at left, substituting adjusted cut length measurement.

To cut additional lengths, unroll, smooth out, and tape down enough fabric, right side up. Lay the first cut length, also right side up, on top of the unrolled fabric; carefully position it so that the motifs in the pattern repeats match perfectly. Pin the two layers together to be sure they don't shift. Cut the additional length along the edges of the first one. To avoid confusion later, use chalk or pins to mark the heading or hem of each length where you want full repeats to fall.

Squaring off the sides. When you match patterns to join widths, you will automatically establish straight, vertical lines down the sides of the fabric, following the print (see page 49, "Joining fabric widths"). You may have to trim seam allowances to make them even.

Depending on how off-grain the print is, side hems might need to be adjusted so that the folded edge runs exactly with the print. To do this, fold the side hem along a vertical line in the print. Then cut away excess fabric so that the hem is even. This might alter the width of your side hem slightly, but it will make the print look square to the floor, window, and ceiling.

Squaring off sides

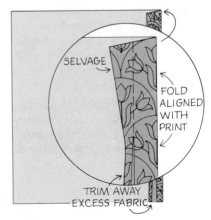

Sewing Simplified

You'll be happy to discover that sewing window treatments is about as simple as sewing can be. Unless you add decorative details, such as a scalloped hem, all stitching runs in straight lines.

Even if your heart is set on ruffles or welting—but you feel daunted by lack of experience—you may find such accents manageable with one of the special sewing machine attachments listed in this section.

Your sewing machine

Those straight lines of stitching should be smooth and flawless—as long as your machine runs well and is carefully attuned to the fabric it will stitch.

If you haven't used the machine for a while, review its manual and lubricate the machine with the oil specified for it.

Preparing for perfect stitching

A line of stitching results from a very intricate performance by the sewing machine. Factors that you control are these: thread and needle size, proper threading of the machine, pressure of the presser foot, thread tension, and stitch length. Study and play with these factors by stitching through two layers of the fabric you will be using. Continue until the stitches look perfect.

Thread and needle. Use needle and thread in sizes that are compatible with the weight of your fabric—fine for lightweight and delicate cloth, medium for medium weight, and heavy-duty for heavy fabric.

Presser foot. Experiment until pressure from the presser foot holds the fabric firmly enough for a smooth stitch, but not so heavily as to leave an indentation on the fabric.

As you sew, gently guide the fabric by placing one hand behind the presser foot and the other hand in front. Without pulling, try to keep the fabric as smooth and flat as possible.

Thread tension. The usual culprit behind untidy stitching and seams that pucker is incorrect thread tension. Properly adjusted thread tension is especially important in sewing the long seams and hems in window coverings—experiment until your stitches are smooth and flat.

Stitch length. Experiment, too, for a good stitch length. Generally, you don't need an extremely strong seam for window coverings; to avoid puckering, it's best to use relatively long stitches.

Helpful attachments

Local stores that sell your brand of machine may stock accessories for your model that could greatly ease special stitching situations.

Buttonhole attachment. If the feed dog of your machine can be lowered, you can use a buttonholer to tack pleats. You'll need to use a sturdy needle.

Ruffler. A specialized gathering foot, it performs quickly and efficiently to gather a long ruffle.

Roller foot. If your fabric is slippery, this special foot may help. It grips the top layer of fabric, keeping it evenly fed with the bottom layer.

Zipper foot. Designed to stitch alongside a thickness that would obstruct the regular presser foot, a zipper foot is used both to make cording and to attach it to the edge of a hem.

Seam gauge. This attachment can be set at different distances from the needle as a guide in sewing various seam and hem widths.

A tape trick

Ordinary household masking tape can serve as a handy guide for keeping long seams and hems straight and parallel with the edges of the fabric during stitching.

As shown below, you simply measure to the right of the needle the distance required for seams or hems. Place a 6-inch strip of tape with its lefthand edge at this point, parallel to the line of stitching. As you sew, keep the seam allowance (or edge of the hem) lined up with the edge of the tape. Even if your machine has its own seam guide markings, you're likely to find this longer tape guide a more effective aid to straight stitching.

In placing the strip of tape for a wide hem, measure 1/8 inch less than the width of the hem. This way, the stitches will run just inside the inner fold of the hem.

A tape trick

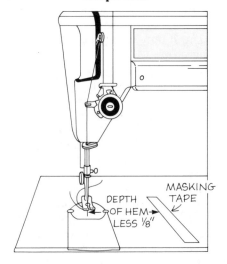

DEPTH OF HEM LESS 1/8"

MASKING TAPE

Making seams and hems

Both seams and hems in window treatments frequently require long, monotonous stitching. To keep the stitching straight and tidy, try to relax and sew at a steady, unhurried pace.

Trim selvages

Before you join fabric widths, trim away selvages. Otherwise, as the body of the fabric "relaxes" after the covering is hung, the relatively dense, tightly woven selvages will cause puckering. (On fabrics that tend to ravel, though, just clip through the selvages about every 2 inches.)

Joining fabric widths

Sometimes you must seam together one or more full fabric widths plus a quarter—or other fractional—width, to obtain your total width.

For neatest appearance, full widths of fabric should hang in the center of curtains and shades, as well as cornices and flat valances. Place additional full or partial fabric widths on the sides of the central unbroken width. Consult the drawings and sketch a plan for your window

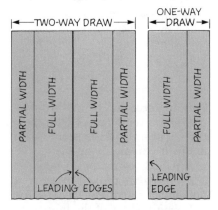

←—TWO-WAY DRAW—→

PARTIAL WIDTH | FULL WIDTH | FULL WIDTH | PARTIAL WIDTH

LEADING EDGES

ONE-WAY ←—DRAW—→

FULL WIDTH | PARTIAL WIDTH

LEADING EDGE

←—SINGLE PANEL—→

PARTIAL WIDTH | FULL WIDTH | PARTIAL WIDTH

based on the number of fabric widths you need.

In the case of draperies, join full or partial widths wherever they will be hidden inside a seam.

Fabric in window treatments always hangs lengthwise, because it naturally drapes best when sewn in the direction of the lengthwise grain. Additionally, the fabric is more stable and resists sagging when the lengthwise grain hangs vertically.

To join unpatterned fabrics you can use plain, French, or self-bound seams.

For patterned fabrics, plain seams are best. You must match the motifs on each piece as you lay the fabric widths on top of one another, right sides together. To do this, carefully pin through the same spot on a design motif from each layer to assure proper alignment of the pattern. Then stitch together in a plain seam, using a 1/2-inch seam allowance.

Finishes for plain seams. Any fabric that you can see through when lined (hold both fabrics up to the light to be sure) and any that will be used unlined should have neat, clean seam edges. Also, ravel-prone fabrics are more durable if the edges are finished.

You can quickly trim the seam allowances of tightly woven fabrics with saw-toothed or scalloped pinking shears. But for a more professional job, use your sewing machine to zigzag seam allowances together, 1/8 inch from the line of stitching. Then trim the excess fabric away along the edge of the zigzag stitching.

French seam. Especially recommended for sheer fabrics and any unlined treatment is the French seam. As shown on the next page, it leaves a finished edge that will look inconspicuous should it show through the face of the fabric.

With wrong sides together, *stitch ¼ inch from edge.*

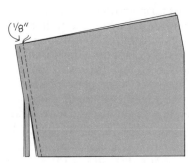

Trim seam allowance *to ⅛ inch; open fabric and press seam allowance to one side.*

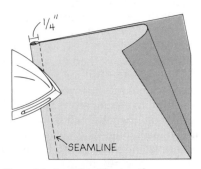

Turn fabric *right sides together, enclosing ⅛-inch seam allowance; stitch ¼ inch from edge. Press.*

Self-bound seam. If you want seams that are simpler to sew than French seams but still neat and finished-looking, you might prefer the self-bound seam, shown at the top of the next column.

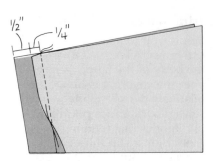

With right sides together, *position top layer of fabric ½ inch from edge of bottom layer. Stitch ¾ inch from edge of bottom layer.*

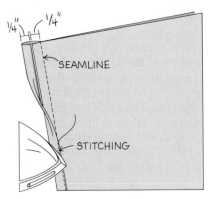

Fold and press *seam allowance of bottom layer to meet edge of top layer; fold and press again, just covering first stitching. Stitch close to fold.*

Pressing seams. The method of pressing a seam varies with the type of seam and the seam finish, if any. If you are using plain, unfinished seams, or if seam allowances are pinked to prevent raveling, press them open—provided both sides of the fabric are the same color. On fabrics with a darker right side and lighter wrong side, press the seams to one side; do the same with seams having a zigzag finish. Press French and self-bound seams to one side and, because they pucker slightly when sewn, gently pull them straight as you press.

Turning hems

Hems in window coverings are usually doubled; half the hem allowance is folded under to the wrong side, then folded the same distance again.

Usually the simplest way to make the double fold is to press it in place. Use a hem gauge to measure the width of each fold. Unless specified otherwise in a project, side hems are 1½ inches wide (3 inches total) and bottom hems are 3 or 4 inches wide (6 or 8 inches total).

Basting hems. If a fabric has a loose weave or is particularly heavy, it may stretch noticeably after hanging. For this reason, professionals hang most draperies (and some curtains) from some high point for several days before permanently sewing bottom hems. To achieve the same result, merely baste the bottom hem and hang the drapery or curtain at the window. After a week or so, mark any needed adjustments (it may not be necessary to undo the entire hem), take the treatment down, and do the final stitching of the hem. Finally, tack the side seams in the vicinity of the hem, if they've been disturbed in the process.

Stitching hems. Depending on the finish you prefer, you can blindstitch hems by hand or by machine (consult your manual) —or you can simply run a line of straight machine stitching close to the first fold line.

A trial run of stitching through three thicknesses of scrap fabric will show whether you need to adjust the machine for the added layer. Testing a sample will also give you a chance to correct a common problem in straight-stitching hems—sometimes the machine gradually pushes the folded hem ahead of the base layer of fabric so that, at the end of the hemline, the fabric layers are no longer aligned. If this happens, loosen the pressure of the presser foot slightly. Also, slow down your stitching.

How to Make
Curtains

Curtains tend to be simple—they flutter in a gentle breeze and can be pushed aside by helping hands. Best of all, curtains are easy and fun to make. Even if you've never before tried sewing for windows, you're sure to find a curtain style here that's ideal for your first project.

Versatile window coverings

Adaptable to many different decorative styles, curtains are extremely versatile window coverings. They can cover all or only part of a window—depending on how much light and privacy you want. You can combine them with draperies or shades, if you like, for added insulation or for a dramatic decorative effect.

Once you've selected the style you want to make (projects start on page 56), be sure to go over the step-by-step instructions carefully—even reading them twice. Also be sure to review pages 36–47 for information on measuring for, buying, and preparing fabric.

A look at hardware

You'll find an intriguing assortment of curtain hardware available in department stores, retail drapery shops, and many large fabric stores—particularly those specializing in decorator fabrics.

Like solving the chicken-or-the-egg riddle, deciding which should come first—selecting hardware or selecting fabric—is tricky. It is important to choose hardware that complements your chosen fabric, as well as the style of the curtain and the room where it will hang. But it is virtually impossible to determine the amount of fabric you'll need until you've positioned the hardware or marked its position with pencil at your window. Probably the most practical solution is to take with you samples of the fabrics you're considering when you shop for hardware.

Listed here are the most common types of curtain hardware. Stores can usually order for you any items they do not have in stock.

Rods

Flat curtain rods. These adjustable rods attach with brackets to the wall or window frame. Use them for full-length or café curtains (or valances) that are either gathered on the rod or hung with oval rings or valance hooks.

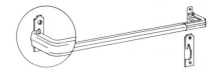

Double flat rods. These are designed for double curtain treatments, such as criss-cross ruffled

curtains or a curtain plus valance. Because the return on the outside rod is longer than that on the inside rod, you can hang one curtain directly in front of another. The rods adjust in length and attach to the wall with a double bracket.

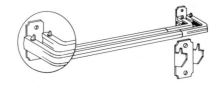

Corner and bay window rods. These two or three-piece adjustable flat rods are hinged for use on corner-meeting windows or angled bays.

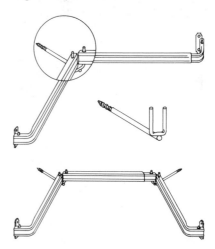

Café rods. This term covers quite a range of styles, from simple, round brass rods to larger, more decorative fluted rods with ornate finials. They attach with brackets to the wall or frame, and most are adjustable in length. Use these for café or full-length curtains that are either gathered on the rod or hung with rings.

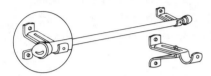

Wood poles. Paired with large matching rings and supported by decorative brackets, wood poles are distinctive with floor-length curtains (though usually too heavy-looking for café styles). They are available in various lengths (or can be cut to size) and finishes.

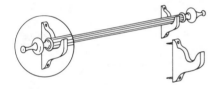

Sash rods. Commonly used on French doors and casement windows to hold sash curtains (sometimes called casement or stretch curtains) or hourglass curtains, these adjustable rods attach with brackets to the top and bottom of the frame.

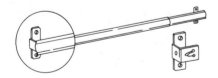

Tension rods. Oval or round, these rods have a spring-tension mechanism inside to hold rod and curtain within the window frame. Often they are the only practical choice for recessed windows.

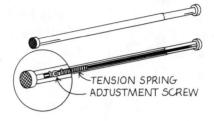

Custom-bent, cut-to-fit rods. For use on vertical curves such as arched windows, these round rods are sometimes made of brass, usually of aluminum. Many custom drapery shops have hardware suppliers who will bend rods to order.

Accessories

Wood sockets. Use these with wood poles for inside-the-frame installation. The sockets are screwed into the frame; the rod slips inside.

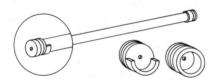

Finials. These eye-catching end pieces dress up a wood pole.

Extension brackets. These attach to ordinary brackets to extend the length of the rod return—a feature sometimes needed to allow multiple-tier curtains to hang freely.

Extension plate. With this metal plate attached to the window frame, you can mount brackets beyond the frame without having to put holes in the wall.

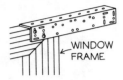

Screws and bolts. Use screws in predrilled holes to secure brackets to window frame or wall stud. If brackets will be attached between studs on a hollow gypsum board or plaster wall, you'll need expansion bolts or toggle bolts. For more detailed information on screws and bolts, refer to "Use the right fastener," page 78.

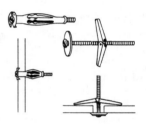

Weights. Inserted in hems or tacked in lower corners, weights may be just what you need to make a tailored treatment hang crisply or to keep a lightweight panel from billowing in the breeze or drawing up at the seams. Read "Weighting lower hems," page 64, to see how to attach these tiny but highly effective accessories.

Rings and hooks

Clip-on rings. Easy to attach at the outset and easy to remove when the curtain needs cleaning, clip-on rings grip the curtain with spring-action prongs. You can find them in metal or plastic (less likely to cut threads), in round or oval styles, and in a range of sizes. Clip-on rings may not be strong enough to bear the weight of full-length curtains.

Plain rings. Made of metal, wood, or plastic, these rings are hand-stitched to the top of the curtain, then slid onto the rod.

Eyelet rings. These rings can be sewn to the curtain's top edge. Or, if the eyelets are large enough, they can be coupled with drapery hooks; the hook, which is secured to the curtain's heading, slips through the eyelet.

Hooks. Pinned directly into the curtain heading, valance hooks (left) fit over the rod; regular drapery hooks (right) slip through the eyelets of eyelet rings.

Pleater hooks. The prongs fit into slots in pleater tape, creating a simple pinched pleat. Then the hook fits through an eyelet—or, in the combination version, an

attached ring slips onto a round curtain rod.

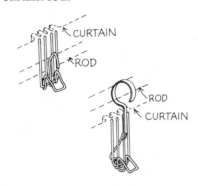

Rod placement

Begin with the rule that a rod must always be perfectly level (even when the window is not) for any treatment to hang properly. Beyond that, the exact position of your curtain rod is up to you. It will depend on what you want the curtain to cover and on how you want it to look from outside.

The usual position for full-length curtains, for valances, or for the top tier of multiple cafés is between the outer corners of the frame—or just outside the opening on a recessed or metal-frame window. Place the rod about five inches above the glass if you want the heading to be concealed from outside. If you'll be placing several rods on a window for café tiers, the guidelines on pages 54–55 will help.

You can camouflage the size or shape of a window by placing rods well above the frame or by extending them to some point on the wall at each side. Or you might prefer to leave the frame exposed, with rods placed close to the glass or even between the jambs.

If you plan to open and close the curtains and you want to expose the entire glass area, you'll need longer rods to allow for stackback (see page 37).

Curtains for French doors or casement windows are usually gathered on sash rods placed just above and below the glass. Securing the fabric at the bottom keeps it from catching when the door or window is closed.

Experiment

Finding the ideal location for your rod may appear to be a straightforward matter. But, beware! Many a minor domestic dispute has been known to arise over those very few inches up, down, to the right, or to the left, when fixtures are placed on family walls. While perhaps not quite so agonizing a decision as where to hang a picture or where to install the can opener in a crowded kitchen, rod placement for a curtain does require forethought.

As an aid to visualizing finished results, it might be a good idea at this point to use shelf paper or wrapping paper and make a mockup of the future window treatment.

To simulate the rod, experiment with strips of masking tape of various lengths; place these at different heights, joining them to your paper "curtains" until you arrive at an arrangement that pleases your eye. Then back away and tour the room so that you can view the window from various angles to see what sort of effect you've created.

Does your window suddenly look wider or squatter? Or does it look surprisingly tall and stately? Have you managed to conceal a frame that had become a tiresome eyesore—or to highlight one that's handsome? Making adjustments now is easy—but problems discovered later could be very difficult to correct.

Keep it on the level

Once you are satisfied that you've found the optimal position for your rod, equip yourself with a carpenter's level to check bracket positions. Even if you do not actually install the brackets before making the curtains, it is quite important to make sure that they will be level. Hammer a small nail lightly into the wall or frame to indicate the top of each bracket. Lay a thin dowel across the nails and check it with the level.

Rod placement for café tiers

As a general rule, when you position rods for café tiers, you'll find that the finished treatment will look best if you divide the window into halves, thirds, or quarters—rather than placing the rods arbitrarily. On paned windows, position rods so that they line up with the muntins (the strips that separate the panes).

You may want to arrange multiple tiers of café curtains so that each one overlaps the rod directly below it by about three inches—creating a soft, undulating effect. However, if you want to show off special headings (scalloped ones, for example, as shown below), each tier should end just short of the one below it.

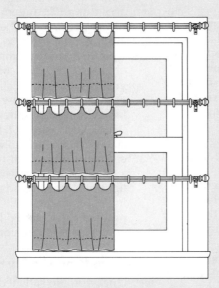

To avoid confusion when measuring for multiple tiers, it's best to install rods at the outset, rather than simply marking their positions with pencil.

Single-tier café curtains usually hang from rods placed so that the upper half, third, or quarter of the glass is exposed. Extending to the sill, apron, or floor, these simple curtains combine beautifully with other treatments: a valance, full-length tied-back curtains, draperies, or even roller shades.

Double or triple-tier café curtains with exposed headings (such as a scalloped treatment) are easy to position.

1. Mount the top rod and measure from the top of the rod (or bottom of a ring, if used) to the point where the lowest tier will end.

2. Divide the result from step 1 by 2 for double tiers, or by 3 for triple tiers. The result from step 2 is the distance between the rods. Measure this distance from the top of the first rod (or the bottom of a ring, if used) to locate the position of the top of the second rod (or bottom of a ring).

3. Mount the second rod; do the same to place and mount the last rod, if making triple tiers.

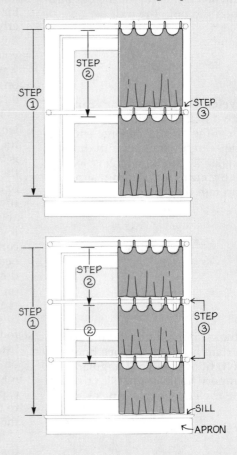

Double or triple tiers that overlap require a few more steps to determine rod positions.

1. Mount the top rod and measure from the top of the rod (or the bottom of a ring, if used) to the desired length of the entire treatment.

2. Divide the result from step 1 by 2 for double tiers, or by 3 for triple tiers, to obtain the visible curtain length of each one.

3. Subtract 3 inches from the result from step 2. This figure is the distance from the top of the upper rod (or bottom of a ring) to the top of the second rod (or bottom of a ring). Mount the second rod.

4. If making triple tiers, measure from the top of the second rod (or bottom of a ring) the distance of the visible curtain length (result from step 2). This is the position of the top of the third rod (or bottom of a ring). Mount the third rod.

2. Divide the result from step 1 by 4 to obtain the visible curtain length of the top tier.

3. Divide the result from step 2 by 3.

4. Add the result from step 3 to the result from step 2. This figure is the visible curtain length of the second tier.

5. Add the result from step 3 to the result from step 4 to find the visible curtain length of the third tier.

6. Subtract 3 inches from the visible curtain length of the uppermost tier (result from step 2). This is the distance from the top of the first rod (or bottom of a ring) to that of the second rod (or bottom of a second ring). Mount the second rod.

7. The distance from the top of the second rod to the top of the third rod (or between bottoms of rings) is equal to the visible curtain length of the second tier (result from step 4). Mount the third rod.

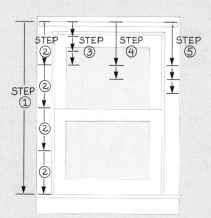

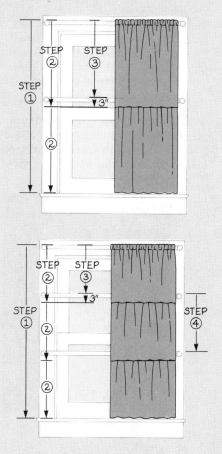

Triple tiers in graduated lengths are usually positioned so that the lengths increase proportionately from top to bottom.

1. Mount the top rod and measure from its top (or bottom of a ring, if used) to the point where the lowest tier will end.

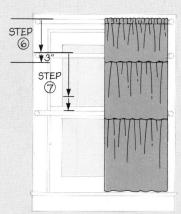

Café curtains

Perhaps the invention of a clever French restaurateur, the first café curtains were an ingenious way to decorate streetside windows. Only the lower portion of the window was covered, assuring seated patrons of privacy, while allowing passersby a glimpse of the tempting atmosphere within.

Such a good and novel idea was bound to catch on. The basic café curtain—suspended from a rod and covering only part of the window—has evolved into a wardrobe of styles which lend themselves to windows throughout the house.

A single-tier treatment with matching valance can perk up a not-so-sunny kitchen window. Cafés paired with ruffled tiebacks make a soft, graceful bedroom treatment—providing privacy while letting in sunshine.

You can make these cheerful café curtains with any one of a host of different top treatments: rings, rod pockets, scallops, pleats, or even pleats and scallops combined. The directions are all here —just pick a style and sew.

Basic café curtains

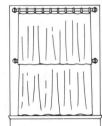

Simple and speedy to sew, this style makes a good rainy-day project—you can spruce up the kitchen windows while you wait for the sun to shine in.

You can use the same instructions to make multiple tiers (see "Rod placement for café tiers," pages 54–55).

You'll need three rings for every 12 inches of flat panel width. The rings can be sewn on, clipped on, or paired with drapery hooks.

For a two-panel treatment, just double the side hem allowances given below and repeat procedure for second panel. For a lined treatment, see instructions for "Basic sack lining," page 67.

Hem allowances for one panel:

Lower hem	6 inches
Side hems	6 inches total
Top hem	2 inches

1. **Measure for, buy, and prepare fabric** (see pages 36-47). Join widths if necessary.

2. **Lower hem.** Turn up lower edge 3 inches, wrong sides together; press. Fold over another 3 inches and press again. Blind-stitch by hand or straight-stitch by machine close to edge of first fold; press.

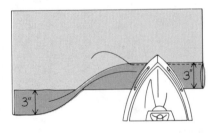

3. **Side hems.** Turn, press, and stitch side hems as in step 2, making each fold 1½ inches wide.

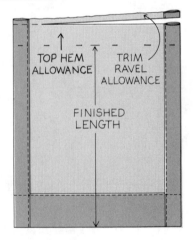

4. **Mark finished length.** On right side, measure from lower edge up panel a distance equal to finished length; mark this distance with a pin about every 4 inches across panel.

5. **Trim upper edge.** Measure and mark proper top hem allowance above pin-marked finished length line, and trim away ravel allowance.

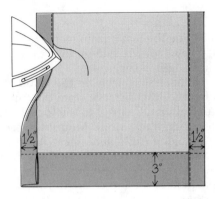

6. **Turn top hem.** Fold cut edge of fabric, wrong sides together, to meet pin-marked line; press. Make second fold, this time along pin-marked line; remove pins and

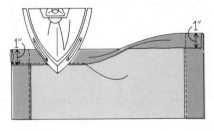

press again. Stitch close to first fold; press.

7. **Attach rings.** At each end of panel, sew or clip a ring to the top edge of hem—or insert the point of a 1-inch drapery hook 1⅜ inches below edge and attach eyelet ring. Space additional rings (or hooks and rings) between, about 4 inches apart.

Rod-pocket café curtains

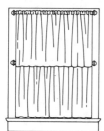

With this simple, cheerful style, you won't need rings or hooks. You simply adjust the size of the top hem of the basic café, making it serve as a snug pocket for the rod.

For a two-panel treatment, just double the side hem allowances and repeat procedure for second panel. For a lined treatment, see instructions for "Enclosed lining," page 65.

Hem allowances for one panel:

Lower hem   6 inches
Side hems   6 inches total
Top hem   Circumference
                     of rod+ 1½ inches

1. **Follow steps 1–6** for "Basic café curtains" on opposite page.

2. **Insert rod** between back 2 layers of rod pocket and gather curtain evenly over length of rod (or half of rod for 2-panel treatment).

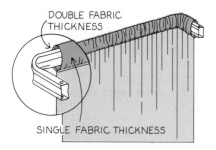

DOUBLE FABRIC THICKNESS

SINGLE FABRIC THICKNESS

Rod-pocket curtains with headings

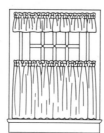

A heading above the pocket on a rod-pocket style forms an instant ruffle as the rod is inserted. This extra flurry of fabric can look as nostalgic as Grandmother's parlor—or quite contemporary—depending on your choice of fabric.

For a two-panel treatment, just double the side hem allowance given below and repeat procedure for second panel. For a lined treatment, see "Enclosed lining," page 65.

Hem allowances for one panel:

Lower hem   6 inches
Side hems   6 inches total
Top hem   Circumference
                     of rod+ 1½ inches
                     + 2 times desired
                     width of heading

1. **Follow steps 1–5** for "Basic café curtains" on opposite page.

2. **Turn top hem.** Fold 1½ inches from cut edge of fabric, wrong sides together; press. Make second fold, this time along pin-marked line; remove pins and press again. Stitch close to first fold.

3. **Mark heading.** Measure down from the top edge a distance equal to the width for the heading; mark point with pin.

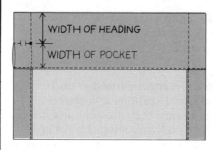

WIDTH OF HEADING

WIDTH OF POCKET

4. **Stitch pocket.** Place curtain panel under presser foot so that pin-marked spot is directly under needle and top edge is to the right of the needle. Lower presser foot and remove pin. Set hem

gauge attachment to width of heading, or apply a strip of masking tape across base of machine (see "A tape trick," page 48). Stitch across panel parallel to top hem edge.

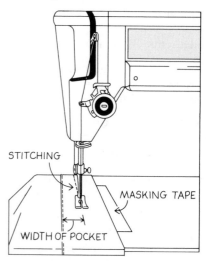

STITCHING

MASKING TAPE

WIDTH OF POCKET

5. **Insert rod through pocket** between back 2 layers of fabric. Gather curtain evenly over length of rod, or half of rod for 2-panel treatment.

Sash café curtains

Gathered on two rods, then stretched between them, sash cafés are a simple variation of the preceding rod-pocket styles. They can be made with or without headings. Sash curtains are a practical choice for casement windows and French doors; the lower rod keeps the fabric from catching when the window or door is closed.

For a two-panel treatment, just double the side hem allowance and repeat the procedure for the second panel. For a lined treatment, see "Special sack lining," page 70.

(Continued on next page)

Hem allowances for one panel:

Lower hem	Circumference of rod + 1½ inches + 2 times desired width of heading, if used
Top hem	Same as lower hem
Side hems	6 inches

1. **Measure for, buy, and prepare fabric** (see pages 36-47). Join widths if necessary.

2. **Side hems.** Turn in one side edge 1½ inches, wrong sides together; press. Fold over another 1½ inches and press again. Stitch close to first fold; press. Repeat procedure for opposite side.

3. **Lower hem.** Turn up lower edge ½ the hem allowance, wrong sides together; press. Make a second fold equal to the first and press again. Stitch close to first fold.

4. Follow steps **4–6** for "Basic café curtains," page 56. (If you want to make sash curtains with headings, at this point follow steps 2–4 for "Rod-pocket curtains with headings," page 57, stitching upper and lower rod pockets.)

5. **Insert rods** through pockets between back 2 layers of fabric. Gather curtain evenly over rods (or half of rods for 2-panel treatment).

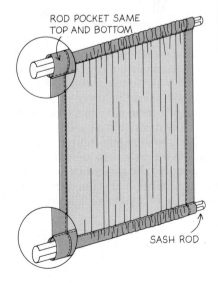

ROD POCKET SAME TOP AND BOTTOM

SASH ROD

Scalloped café curtains

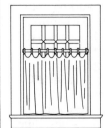

A scalloped edge running along the top of a café curtain gives it a softly tailored look. Scalloped curtains have less fullness, so they require less fabric than other styles. When calculating total yardage, multiply by 1½, instead of 2½, for fullness.

For added body, particularly with lightweight fabrics, you might want to stiffen the scallops with a band of crinoline or buckram. To do so, follow steps 1–4 for "Pleated and scalloped café curtains," page 62; then continue with step 2, below (omitting steps 4 and 5). However, if your curtain will also be lined, check lining instructions first (see below).

You'll need a ring for each space between scallops and one for each end. Or use 12-inch lengths of ribbons.

For a two-panel treatment, just double the side hem allowance given below and repeat procedure for second panel. For a lined treatment, follow steps 1–9 for "Enclosed lining," page 65, then proceed to step 2, below.

Hem allowances for one panel:

Lower hem	6 inches
Side hems	6 inches total
Top hem	Depth of scallop + 4 inches

1. **Follow steps 1–5** for "Basic café curtains," page 56, but in step 4 place pins in *wrong* side of fabric.

2. **Determine number and width of scallops and spaces.** To be sure they are centered on the panel, you should have an odd number of scallops. It's best to keep their diameter to 4 to 6 inches.

Subtract 3 inches (for side hems) from flat panel width (on a 28-inch-wide panel, for example, 28 − 3 = 25) to find the width of the panel that will be taken up in scallops and spaces.

Divide this result by the approximate scallop width (we'll use 5 inches, for example, so 25 ÷ 5 = 5 scallops).

Spaces between scallops should be no wider than ½ to 1 inch. The number of spaces will be one less than the number of scallops. Multiply the number of spaces (4, in our example) by the desired width (we'll use ½ inch, so 4 × ½ = 2).

Subtract this result from the width that will be taken up in scallops and spaces (25 − 2 = 23).

Divide this result by the number of scallops to find the actual scallop diameter (23 ÷ 5 = about 4½ after rounding to the nearest ¼ inch).

3. **Make paper pattern for scallops.** Cut a strip of wrapping paper or freezer paper 10 inches wide and as long as the flat panel width. Fold paper in half lengthwise, then unfold. Now fold paper in half crosswise and unfold.

Set compass at half the scallop diameter found in step 2 (in our example, at 2¼ for 4½-inch scallops). Place point of compass where foldlines in paper strip intersect. Draw first scallop, starting and ending on lengthwise foldline. Measure spaces, then draw additional scallops to right and left of first one. Continue marking scallops and spaces, ending with a 1½-inch space at each end of pattern.

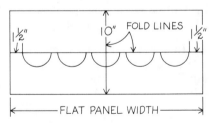

½" ⟶ 10" FOLD LINES ½"

FLAT PANEL WIDTH

Note: If the result of your calculation for scallop width was not an even quarter-inch, but had to be rounded, you may find that you'll need to alter slightly the size of spaces.

4. **Turn top edge of panel** under 1 inch, wrong sides together; press. Stitch close to cut edge of fabric.

5. **Turn top hem** forward along pin-marked line, right sides together. Remove pins and press fold.

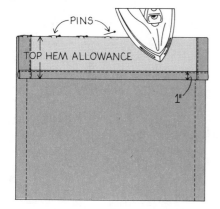

PINS

TOP HEM ALLOWANCE

1"

6. **Pin scallop pattern** to wrong side of fabric, centered on width of panel, matching folded edge of top hem with lengthwise foldline of pattern. Trace scallops onto fabric using tracing wheel and dressmaker carbon. Remove pattern. Pin hem in place before sewing scallops.

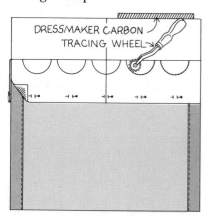

DRESSMAKER CARBON
TRACING WHEEL

7. **Stitch along traced line,** using short stitches and tight tension; remove pins; then cut out scallops, leaving a ¼-inch seam allowance. Clip into seam allowance at intervals, but do not clip through seam. (If your fabric is inclined to

ravel, leave a ½-inch seam allowance and slash at ½ or ¾-inch intervals.)

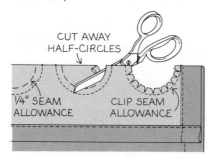
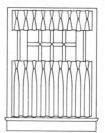

CUT AWAY
HALF-CIRCLES

¼" SEAM
ALLOWANCE

CLIP SEAM
ALLOWANCE

8. **Turn right side out;** press. Slipstitch sides of heading to panel. Tack lower edge of hem to panel.

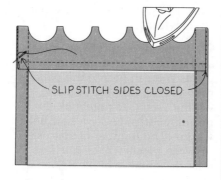

SLIP STITCH SIDES CLOSED

9. **Attach rings or ribbons.** At midpoints between scallops and at each end, sew or clip a ring to edge of fabric—or insert point of 1-inch drapery hook 1⅜ inches below and slip hook through eyelet ring.

If using ribbons in place of rings, fold each 12-inch length in half and stitch folded edge to top edge of panel. Tie bows over rod.

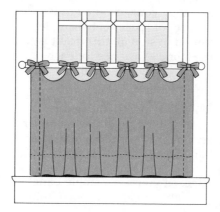

Pleated café curtains

A traditional pleated heading lends a note of formality to the usually casual café style. And to top it off, a pleated valance— actually just an abbreviated version of the pleated café curtain (see "Cornices and valances," page 84).

These instructions are for treatments hung from flat curtain rods. If you plan to use a café rod, substitute "3½ inches" for "rod return length" in steps 8 and 9, following.

For pleated treatments, you can manage with a bit less yardage than usual—multiply the finished width by 2¼ for fullness, rather than by 2½.

For each end of a one-panel treatment and for every pleat you'll need a 1-inch drapery hook or a curtain ring (sew-on or clip-on type)— or use an eyelet-ring-and-hook combination. For a two-panel treatment, you'll need one less drapery hook, because one end overlaps another at the center. You'll also need a strip of 3 or 4-inch-wide stiffener (buckram or crinoline) 4½ inches shorter than the total width.

For a two-panel treatment, just double the side hem allowance given below and repeat procedure for second panel. For a lined treatment, follow steps 1–9 for "Enclosed lining," page 65; then proceed to step 2 below.

Hem allowances for one panel:

Top hem	6 inches (with 3-inch stiffener) or 8 inches (with 4-inch stiffener)
Side hems	6 inches total
Lower hem	Same as for top hem

1. **Follow steps 1–4** for "Basic café curtains," page 56, but in step 4, mark finished length on *wrong* side.

2. **Position stiffener.** Fold under one end of stiffener 1 inch; place stiffener on panel, wrong sides together, with folded end ¼ inch from side of panel. Align lower edge of stiffener with pin-marked line and pin stiffener in place.

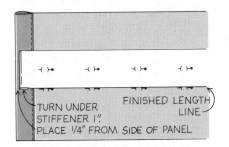

TURN UNDER STIFFENER 1"
PLACE ¼" FROM SIDE OF PANEL

FINISHED LENGTH LINE

Smooth out remainder of stiffener to opposite end; fold under 1 inch and position fold ¼ inch from side of panel as above. Remove pins at finished length line.

3. **Turn top hem.** Measure top hem allowance above stiffener; trim off ravel allowance so hem allowance above stiffener is equal to width of stiffener. Remove pins from stiffener and fold allowance over it; press. Then fold along finished length line and press again; pin in place.

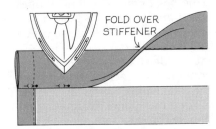

FOLD OVER STIFFENER

4. **Close sides of top hem.** With stiffener in place, stitch sides of hem closed, ⅛ inch from folded edges. Backstitch each end to close side hems securely. To hold

stiffener in place, stitch a second row, parallel to the first and 1¼ inches from folded edges.

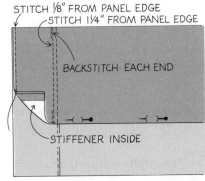

STITCH ⅛" FROM PANEL EDGE
STITCH 1¼" FROM PANEL EDGE
BACKSTITCH EACH END
STIFFENER INSIDE

5. **Subtract finished width** (check your notebook) from flat panel width.

6. **Determine number of pleats and spaces.** To find the number of pleats you can fit into the panel, multiply the number of fabric widths used (see notebook) by 5, for full widths, and by 2 for half widths. The number of spaces between pleats will be one less than the number of pleats.

7. **Size of pleat.** Divide the result from step 5 by the number of pleats that you found in step 6. This figure is the fabric allowance for each pleat. Round off to nearest ¼ inch.

8. **Size of spaces.** For each panel of a two-panel treatment, subtract the rod return length plus 3½ inches from half the finished width; for a single-panel treatment, subtract twice the rod return length.

Divide your result by the number of spaces between pleats (found in step 6); this result is the fabric allowance for each space. Round off the figure to the nearest ¼ inch.

9. **Mark pleats and spaces.** Starting from leading edge (nearest center of window) of each panel in a two-panel treatment, place a pin 3½ inches in from edge. (If yours is a single panel, place the pin at a distance from

the edge equal to the rod return length.) This pin marks the start of the first pleat. Measure and mark the end of the pleat and the space to the next one. Continue across heading until all pleats and spaces are marked with pins —end with a pleat. The portion of flat panel remaining should equal

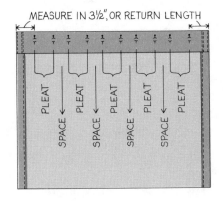

MEASURE IN 3½", OR RETURN LENGTH

PLEAT   SPACE   PLEAT   SPACE   PLEAT   SPACE   PLEAT   SPACE   PLEAT

the rod return length. Because the calculations in steps 7 and 8 were rounded off to the nearest ¼ inch, you may find that you have to adjust pins slightly so that last pleat is positioned on the curve of the rod just before the return. Also, if you have joined fabric widths to make up the panel, it's best to adjust pins so that seams fall close to the edges of pleats. This will make them practically invisible when curtain panel is hung. Be careful not to alter the size of the space when adjusting pins; make adjustments in pleat size only.

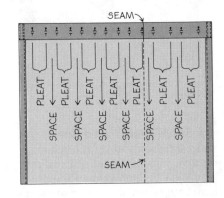

SEAM

PLEAT   SPACE   PLEAT   SPACE   PLEAT   SPACE   PLEAT   SPACE   PLEAT   SPACE   PLEAT   SPACE   PLEAT

SEAM

10. **Make pleats.** On wrong side of heading, match pins at either side of pleat. Lightly finger-press fold. Stitch pleat from bottom of stiffener to top of curtain panel at point where pins meet (stitching line is parallel to fold). Backstitch at each end to hold pleat firmly in place.

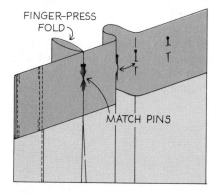

FINGER-PRESS FOLD

MATCH PINS

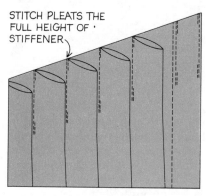

STITCH PLEATS THE FULL HEIGHT OF STIFFENER

Fold large loop into 3 smaller, even loops.

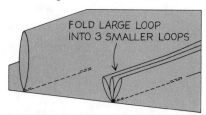

FOLD LARGE LOOP INTO 3 SMALLER LOOPS

Starting at the base of the pleat, stitch the loops in place through fabric and stiffener, as follows: Insert needle ¼ inch from fold of pleat and ¼ inch from bottom of stiffener. Stitch across pleat as shown in next column.

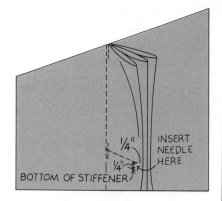

¼"
¼"

INSERT NEEDLE HERE

BOTTOM OF STIFFENER

Some professionals spray a small amount of silicone lubricant on the fabric and the needle to reduce friction and ease the passage of the needle through the fabric. (Look for silicone spray in hardware stores. Be sure to test a small sample on your fabric first.)

If you have a zigzag machine that can attach buttons, you can use this feature to secure pleats. Position the needle as above, set machine controls for attaching buttons, and tack pleat.

Some machines cannot stitch through 18 layers of fabric and 6 of stiffener. If your machine just won't stitch through the pleat, you'll need to tack the pleat by hand. A sturdy needle and a thimble are necessary to push through the thickness of the pleat.

After pleats are stitched, finger-press the folds above the stitching.

11. **Attach rings or drapery hooks.** Either sew or clip a ring to top center of each pleat. Or, pin a drapery hook to back of pleat so that it pierces stiffener, but not the face fabric. (You can also use an eyelet ring to link with the drapery hook.) The top of the hook should be ½ inch down from the top of the curtain, so the point of a 1-inch hook should be inserted 1½ inches from top.

For a one-panel treatment, sew, clip, or pin a drapery hook to each end of panel. For a two-panel treatment, insert drapery hooks as above, at both ends of one panel and at outer end of the other. When you hang the curtain, the panel without the drapery hook overlaps the other.

Cafés with pleater tape

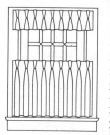

Special tape and special drapery hooks that draw fabric into three folds can automatically pleat your panel for you. While the pleats will not have quite the elegantly finished look of stitched pleats, they are definitely faster and simpler to make.

These instructions are for treatments hung from flat curtain rods. If you plan to use a café rod, substitute "3½ inches" for "rod return length" in step 2.

When calculating for yardage, you can slightly reduce the usual fullness allowance—multiply by 2¼ instead of 2½.

For a one-panel treatment, you'll need a regular drapery hook for each end of the panel. For a two-panel treatment, you'll need only 3 regular drapery hooks because one end overlaps the other at the center. You'll also need a special 4-pronged hook for each pleat, whether the treatment has one or two panels. Finally, you'll need a strip of 3 or 4-inch-wide pleater tape as long as the flat panel width of the curtain.

For a two-panel treatment, just double the side hem allowance given below and repeat procedure for second panel. For a lined treatment, follow steps 1–7 (omitting step 4) of "Basic sack lining," page 67.

Hem allowances for one panel:

Lower hem	6 inches (with 3-inch pleater tape) or 8 inches (with 4-inch pleater tape)
Side hems	6 inches total
Top hem	½ inch

1. **Follow steps 1-2** for "Basic café curtains," page 56, substituting a 4-inch-wide double lower hem if using 4-inch-wide pleater tape.

(Continued on next page)

2. **Attach pleater tape.** Center pleater tape at top of panel, right sides together, 3 inches from each side. Top edges should align and pocket openings on tape should be on the bottom. The distance from the side edge to the first pleat should equal the rod return length plus 3 inches. Stitch tape to panel, ¼ inch from upper edge. Fold tape to wrong side of panel so seamline is ¼ inch down from upper edge; press. Pin tape to panel and stitch ¼ inch from lower edge, taking care not to stitch pockets closed.

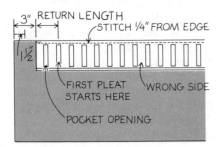

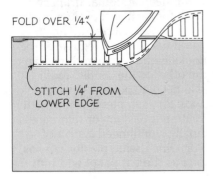

3. **Side hems.** Turn under 1½ inches on each side edge, wrong sides together; press. Turn under another 1½ inches and press again. Stitch close to edge of first fold.

4. **Attach hooks.** Insert 4-pronged hooks into pockets of tape to form pleats. At each end of panel, insert point of 1-inch drapery hook 1½ inches from

top edge for a one-panel treatment. For a two-panel treatment, insert drapery hooks at both ends of one panel and at outer end of the other. When you hang curtain, panel without drapery hook overlaps the other.

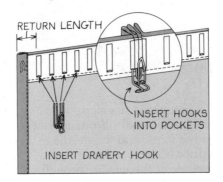

Pleated and scalloped cafés

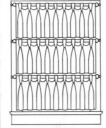

The combination of stately pleats and gentle curves in this decorative heading creates an eye-catching contrast. This treatment is designed to be hung on a café rod, since a flat curtain rod would be revealed by the scallops.

You'll need for each end of panel and for every pleat a 1-inch drapery hook or a curtain ring or an eyelet-ring-and-hook combination. You'll also need a strip of 4-inch-wide stiffener (buckram or crinoline) 4½ inches shorter than the total width.

For a two-panel treatment, just double the side hem allowance given below and repeat procedure for second panel. For a lined treatment, follow steps 1–9 for "Enclosed lining," page 65, then continue with step 2 below.

Hem allowances for one panel:

Bottom hem	8 inches
Side hems	6 inches total
Top hem	4½ inches

1. **Follow steps 1–5** for "Basic café curtains," page 56, but, in step 4, mark finished length on *wrong* side. Substitute proper hem allowances.

2. **Position stiffener.** Turn under 1 inch on each end of stiffener; press. Lay panel wrong side up on table. Center stiffener on top so that lower edge of stiffener overlaps top edge of panel by ½ inch and folded ends face down; pin in place. Stitch ¼ inch from lower edge of stiffener; remove pins.

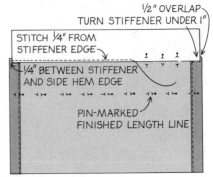

3. **Stitch stiffener to ends.** Fold stiffener forward onto wrong side of panel to meet pin-marked finished length line; press. Stitch ends of stiffener to panel ¼ inch from folded edge; remove pins.

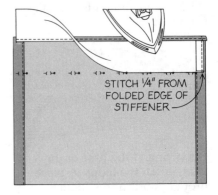

4. **Turn stiffener** to right side of panel along finished length line; pin.

A fan of fabric

To attach the soft, gathered fabric fan shown in the window arches on page 22, you'll need a special curved rod. Order one bent and cut for your window from a custom drapery shop; try to have one of their professionals help you measure for and install the rod.

Use a lightweight, sheer fabric for this treatment, so you can fuss and fold the fabric into shape with ease.

With rod installed, use a steel tape measure to measure the curve of the arch—this figure is the finished width. To find the finished length, measure from the center of the horizontal crosspiece to the farthest point on the arch (if the crosspiece defines a perfect half-circle, with all points on the arch equidistant from its center, simply measure from the center to one side).

Multiply the finished width by 2½ for full-

ness, then add to that 6 inches for side hems. To the finished length, add the top hem allowance specified in "Rod-pocket café curtains" (or in "Rod-pocket curtains with headings" if you want a frill above the rod pocket), both on page 57. Also add to the finished length 8 inches for the fabric "chignon" at the center of the lower edge of the treatment.

To make the panel, simply fold, press, and stitch double 1½-inch side hems. Then make a rod pocket or rod pocket with heading as described on page 57. Slip the rod into the pocket and mount the rod at the window.

To make the fabric chignon, gather the fabric together at the lower center, securing it tightly with a rubber band. Manipulate the free edges of fabric, folding them back and tucking them under the rubber band (trim excess fabric, if necessary) until the chignon is shaped to your liking. Then tie matching embroidery thread tightly just behind the rubber band, and clip the rubber band free.

5. Follow steps 5–7 for "Pleated café curtains," page 60.

6. Size of spaces. For each panel, subtract 3 inches from the finished width. Divide the result by the number of spaces between pleats (found in step 6 of "Pleated café curtains," page 60). This figure, rounded off to the nearest ¼ inch, is the fabric allowance for each space.

7. Mark pleats and spaces. Starting at one end of the panel, place a pin 1½ inches in from edge. This marks the start of the first pleat. Measure and mark the end of the pleat and the space to the next one. Continue across heading until all pleats and spaces are marked with pins—end with a pleat 1½ inches from edge of panel. Because calculations for sizes of pleats and spaces were rounded off to the nearest ¼ inch, you may find that you have to alter slightly the size of pleats. Also, if you have joined fabric widths to make up the panel, it's best to adjust pins to

alter pleat size so that seams fall close to the edges of the pleats.

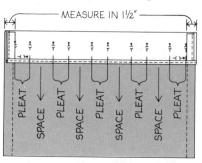

8. Make scallops. Set compass at half the width of space between pleats. With point of compass at top edge of stiffener, midway between 2 pleats, draw scallops on stiffener with light pencil. Stitch as marked; cut out scallops, leaving a ¼-inch seam allowance. Clip into seam allowance but not through stitching. (If your fabric is inclined to ravel, leave a ½-inch seam allowance and slash at ½ or ¾-inch intervals.)

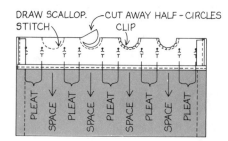

9. Turn heading right side out; press. Stitch facing to side hems, ¼ inch from edge. Backstitch at top and bottom to hold stiffener firmly in place.

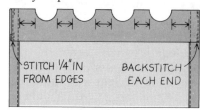

10. Follow steps 10–11 for "Pleated café curtains," page 61, to make pleats between scallops and at ends, and to attach rings or drapery hooks. Note: This style doesn't overlap. For 2-panel treatments, you'll need a ring or hook for each end of both panels.

Full-length curtains

A full-length curtain is exactly what its name implies—a curtain that runs the full length of the window. But a full-length curtain can go beyond the window frame—it can extend down to the floor or up to the ceiling.

You can make a full-length curtain in any number of styles. Café styles that convert to full-length are rod-pocket, rod-pocket with heading, sash, and pleated (see below). Two styles unique to full-length are multiple shirred headings and hourglass. Though full-length curtains are often tied back, they can be left to fall free.

Tieback curtains can be teamed successfully with other treatments—in particular, sash curtains, roller shades, Roman shades, and cafés. And you can top off your full-length curtains with a valance or cornice. Probably the most traditional combination is the pairing of sheer curtains with luxurious draperies.

From café length to full length

With adjusted measurements, most café styles detailed on pages 56–63 can be constructed as a full-length curtain. Here are the changes you'll need to make in the directions given for café styles.

Weighting lower hems

Full-length panels need extra weight at the lower edge to make them hang straight without flaring. To add weight, you should make lower hems 4 inches wide (instead of the 3 inches for café styles); this requires an 8-inch lower hem allowance. (Note that we recommend using 4-inch-wide stiffener or pleater tape for full-

length pleated curtains. If you can't find this and must settle for a 3-inch width, then you should make your hems 3 inches wide as well.)

For even more stability, you can sew small weights into the lower corners of each panel. Either purchase covered weights or enclose weights in small pockets of fabric, then sew to the panel as shown.

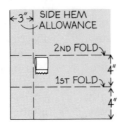

Widening headings

A longer curtain looks better with a wider heading. For headings on pleated styles, use a 4-inch-wide stiffener or pleater tape. Though gathered headings on café curtains (page 57) are usually only an inch or so wide, you can create a very striking effect by designing even wider ones on longer curtains. In general, the longer the curtain, the wider the heading can be and still appear to be in proportion to the rest of the treatment. For a sill-length treatment, you should keep the heading width to 1 or 2 inches, but a floor-to-ceiling curtain can quite effectively carry a 2, 3, or even 4-inch heading if the fabric is stiff enough to stand up.

A simple trick for softening the look of a gathered heading is to sew a heading twice as wide as you would like it to appear at the window. Then, after gathering the finished panel onto the rod, you can make the heading pouf by separating the two thicknesses of fabric (see photograph on page 19).

Covering rods with fabric

Sometimes, rod-pocket curtain panels are used not to cover the glass, but simply to soften the angularity of the window and to add warmth and color to the room. In such a situation, the curtain panels do not meet in the

center, but hang at the sides of the window—either straight down or tied back—from a decorative rod or pole. If the rod doesn't quite suit the fabric—or if you simply want to add spice to the treatment—you might consider covering the rod with a matching sleeve.

Just cut a rectangle of fabric (which you may need to piece together) that is 2½ times as long as the section of the rod you want to cover, with a width equal to the circumference of the rod plus 2½ inches. Sew a single ½-inch hem on each end of the rectangle. Then fold it in half lengthwise, right sides together, and join the unhemmed edges with a ½-inch seam. Turn right side out and gather onto rod or pole, keeping the seam at the back.

To carry this custom touch one step further, you can give the rod sleeve a gathered heading to match those on the curtain panels (see "Rod-pocket curtains with headings," page 57). Simply add the proper heading allowance to the width of the long rectangle. Stitch as explained for a plain gathered rod sleeve. After turning the sleeve right side out, position seam at the back of the pocket and stitch parallel to the top folded edge at a distance equal to the width of the heading. Gather onto rod with the ruffled heading at the top.

Sheer curtains

This understandably popular type of curtain has become a classic window solution over the years—acting as a softening filter against the glass. Sheers subdue bright sunlight, protecting furnishings from fading and fiber breakdown. At the same time, sheers permit delicate veils of light to waft through and fill the room with coziness. Finally, though sheers are translucent, they still provide an effective privacy screen.

Here are a few points to keep in mind when shopping for and working with sheer fabrics:

• Sheer fabrics are made wider than most—up to 118 inches. Using these extra-wide fabrics will usually eliminate the need for joining fabric widths. Their special construction allows them to be turned sideways so that the fabric width runs in the lengthwise direction.

• If you do have to join widths, you should use French seams to conceal raw edges of fabric (see page 49).

• When one or more *full* widths of sheer fabric make up the curtain panel, you may not need to make side hems. The selvages of certain sheer fabrics provide a neat, inconspicuous finish.

• Make double 6-inch lower hems for extra weight to help the panel hang straight and to minimize billowing. A string of bead-like curtain weights (page 52) sewn into the bottom hem will also cut down on fluttering.

• Be extremely careful to make all your cuts absolutely straight. When cut edges are folded into a hem, be certain they are flush with the crease of the fold.

• Because sheer fabrics are usually finely woven, they pucker more easily than other fabrics. Sew with a slightly longer stitch than you would normally use.

Lining methods

Consider the bonuses lining can add to your curtains, and you may well decide that they justify the extra time and expense. Lining enriches the appearance of the treatment while protecting both the face fabric and other fabrics in the room from excessive exposure to sunlight—and lining adds insulation as well.

Here are three different ways to line a curtain panel. The style of curtain you are making will determine the method you choose. Before starting, refer to pages 43 and 45 on lining.

Enclosed lining

Because this type of lining has firm side edges, it is the best choice for scalloped, pleated, and rod-pocket styles. The extra support along the sides will help keep the panel from collapsing below the heading. (If you're using pleater tape, however, follow instructions for "Basic sack lining," page 66.)

Hem allowances for one panel:

	Fabric	Lining
Lower hem	*6–8 inches	4 inches
Side hems	6 inches total	3 inches total
Top hem		
Pleated styles	*4–5 inches	none
Scalloped and rod-pocket styles	same as given under project	none

*Use the smaller figure with 3-inch stiffener, the larger one with 4-inch stiffener.

1. **Measure for, buy, and prepare fabric and lining** (see pages 36–47). Join widths, if necessary, and press seams open.

2. **Lower hems.** With face fabric wrong side up, fold up lower edge a distance equal to ½ the lower hem allowance; press. Fold up the same amount again, and press. Blindstitch by hand, or machine-stitch close to edge of first fold. Repeat for lower hem of lining, making each fold 2 inches deep.

3. **Mark finished length.** On wrong side of face fabric, measure up from the lower edge a distance equal to the finished length (see notebook). Mark with pins about every 4 inches across panel.

4. **Position lining and fabric.** With right sides together, lay lining fabric on top of face fabric so that lower edge of lining is 1 inch above lower edge of face fabric.

A professional trick you can use to prevent lining seams from showing through when panels are hung is to align the first seams from the leading edge of lining

and face fabric. Any slight decrease in fullness this may cause will not be noticed in the finished panel.

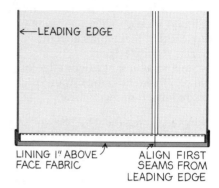

5. **Trim face fabric or lining** as necessary so that lining is 3 inches narrower than face fabric at each side.

6. **Trim upper edges.** Trim away excess fabric along upper edge of lining so that lining edge meets pin-marked finished length line on face fabric. Then, on face fabric, measure and mark proper top hem allowance above finished length line, and trim away ravel allowance.

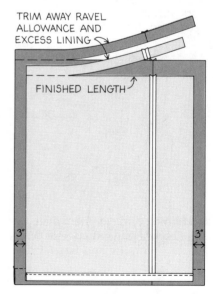

(Continued on next page)

7. Attach lining to side hem. With right sides still together, position lining on face fabric so their edges are aligned at one side (lower edge of lining should still be 1 inch above lower edge of face fabric). Place pins at right angles to side edges.

Start stitching at lower edge of panel, 1½ inches from side. Stitch entire length of face fabric.

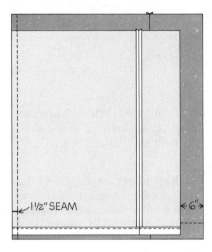

8. Turn first side hem. Separate face fabric from lining, and lay out wrong side up on padded work surface. Press seam toward face fabric along stitching line.

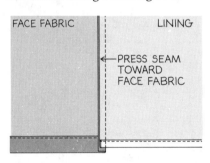

Fold lining and side hem over face fabric along cut edge of seam allowance (lining and face fabric

will now have wrong sides together); press.

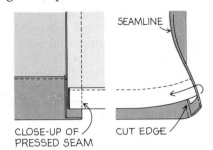

9. Opposite side hem. Unfold fabrics and return them to right-sides-together position, this time aligning remaining side edges of lining and face fabric. Pin and stitch as in step 7. Turn panel right side out. Fold seam in toward center as you did in step 8, so an equal amount of face fabric is showing at each side. Press.

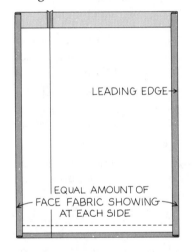

For pleated treatments, proceed with step 2 under "Pleated café curtains," page 59. In step 3, disregard instructions for trimming ravel allowance—you've already done this.

For scalloped styles, proceed with step 2 under "Scalloped café curtains," page 58, or step 2 under "Pleated and scalloped cafés," page 62.

For rod-pocket curtains (with or without headings), fold face fabric, wrong sides together, to meet finished length line; press. Remove pins; then make a second fold, equal to the first, and press. Stitch close to edge of first fold.

For rod-pocket curtains with headings, continue with steps 2–4 on page 57.

Basic sack lining

Used for the basic café, multiple-shirred-heading, tab, and pleater tape styles, this basic sack lining provides a neatly finished backing without adding extra bulk at hems.

Hem allowances for one panel:

	Fabric	Lining
Lower hems	*6–8 inches	4 inches
Side hems	2 inches total	1 inch total
Top hems	½ of figure given under projects (with pleater tape, use ½ inch)	none

*Use the smaller figure with 3-inch pleater tape, the larger one with 4-inch pleater tape.

1. Follow steps 1–4 for "Enclosed lining," page 65. In step 3, mark finished length line on right side of fabric, instead of wrong side.

2. Mark finished length line on lining. With face fabric and lining positioned as in step 4 of "Enclosed lining," pin finished length line on wrong side of lining to match pin-marked line on face fabric underneath.

3. Trim upper edges. On face fabric, measure and mark proper top hem allowance above finished length line, and trim away ravel allowance.

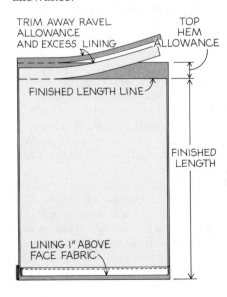

On lining, trim away fabric above finished length line. Remove pins from lining only.

For pleater tape curtains, skip to step 5.

4. **Turn top hems.** Fold the face fabric under, wrong sides together, along finished length line. Remove pins and press.

Fold the lining under, wrong sides together, 1/2 inch and press.

Pin each hem in place separately.

5. **Attach lining to face fabric.** With lining positioned on face fabric, right sides together, align side edges (lining is narrower than face fabric). Lower edge of lining should still be 1 inch above lower edge of face fabric. Pin at right angles to side edges. Starting at bottom of lining, stitch lining to face fabric at sides, making 1-inch seams. For basic café panels, tab, or pleater tape curtains, stop stitching 1/2 inch below top edge of lining. For multiple shirred styles, end stitching at start of heading.

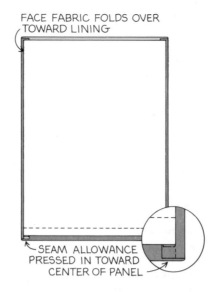

LINING 1" NARROWER THAN FACE FABRIC

STITCH TO 1/2"
BELOW TOP EDGE
OF LINING
OR
START OF
MULTIPLE SHIRRED
HEADING

FINISHED LENGTH

1" SEAM

6. **Turn panel right side out.** When you turn panel, center lining so that an equal amount of face fabric shows on either side of lining (just under 1/2 inch, depending on bulk of fabric). Position seam allowance toward center of panel; press.

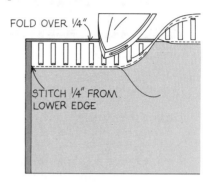

FACE FABRIC FOLDS OVER TOWARD LINING

SEAM ALLOWANCE PRESSED IN TOWARD CENTER OF PANEL

For tab curtains, proceed now to step 2 under "Tab curtains," page 71. For pleater tape curtains, continue with step 7 below. For basic café and multiple-shirred-heading styles, skip to step 8 in next column.

7. **Attach pleater tape to panel.** Center pleater tape at top of panel, with right side of tape facing right side of face fabric. Top edges should align and pocket openings on tape should be on the bottom. The distance from the side edge of panel to the pocket that will begin the first pleat should equal the rod return length. Fold forward and press 1/2 inch on each end of pleater tape and pin in place. Stitch tape to panel 1/4 inch from upper edge. Remove pins from ends of tape, finger-press folds, then fold tape to lining side of panel so seamline is 1/4 inch down from upper edge;

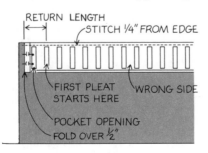

RETURN LENGTH
STITCH 1/4" FROM EDGE
FIRST PLEAT STARTS HERE
WRONG SIDE
POCKET OPENING
FOLD OVER 1/2"

press. Pin tape to panel and stitch 1/4 inch from lower edge of tape, taking care not to stitch pockets closed.

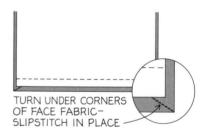

FOLD OVER 1/4"

STITCH 1/4" FROM LOWER EDGE

To complete curtains with pleater tape, see step 4 under "Cafés with pleater tape," page 62.

8. **Attach lining** to face fabric along top edge (for basic café curtain and those with multiple shirred headings). Blindstitch top edge of lining to face fabric, making sure that stitches catch only back layer of face fabric hem and don't show on front.

9. **Turn under lower corners** of face fabric on the diagonal, as shown, and slipstitch in place. Proceed with headings as instructed in individual projects.

TURN UNDER CORNERS OF FACE FABRIC— SLIPSTITCH IN PLACE

(Continued on page 70)

Tiebacks for curtains and draperies

Tiebacks do more than soften the look of a window treatment; they offer a simple means of opening and closing the panels.

Though you can buy decorative cord or chain tiebacks, your options are multiplied if you make your own. Choose a simple-to-make tailored tieback, or vary the theme by adding ruffles. For a distinctive touch, consider encircling the panel with a fabric-covered cord as shown in the photographs on pages 12 and 24. You should make and hang panels before beginning tiebacks.

Tailored tiebacks

For a pair of tiebacks, you'll need fabric, fusible interfacing, four ½-inch-diameter plastic rings, and two cup hooks.

1. Determine finished size of tieback. From scrap fabric, cut a strip 2–4 inches wide and as long as half the finished width of the treatment. Wrap it around one panel and move it up and down, folding under and pinning sides and ends, until you are pleased with the way it looks. With pins, mark desired finished length and width of tieback.

2. Screw cup hooks into wall. With a pencil, lightly mark point on wall where you want to attach

tieback. Mark same point on opposite side of window. Screw cup hooks at these marks.

3. Cut fabric and interfacing. To find cut size of each tieback, add one inch to the finished length; double the finished width and add one inch. Aligning scissors with fabric grain (or with pattern, if off-grain), cut 2 strips to this size. Also, cut 2 strips of fusible interfacing the same size.

4. Iron on interfacing. Center one strip of fusible interfacing on wrong side of each fabric tieback and fuse in place with iron, following manufacturer's instructions.

5. Stitch tieback. Fold tieback in half lengthwise, right sides together. Stitch the length of the strip, ½ inch from cut edge, leaving ends open.

6. Turn right side out and press, having seam run down center (this will be wrong side of tieback). At ends, turn cut edges inside ½ inch; press and blindstitch closed.

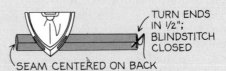

7. Hand-sew plastic rings to back of tieback, centered ¼ inch from each end. Take care not to sew through front layer of fabric.

For a slightly different look, you can press corners to back of tieback, forming points at ends, as shown. Tack corners in place, then sew rings to back of tieback ¼ inch from points.

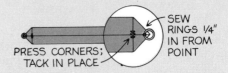

Single-ruffle tiebacks

For a pair of tiebacks, you'll need fabric, four ½-inch-diameter plastic rings and two cup hooks.

1. Determine finished length of tieback as in step 1 of "Tailored tiebacks."

2. Screw cup hooks into wall as in step 2 of "Tailored tiebacks."

3. Make 2 single-edged ruffles, following directions on page 74. Ruffle for each tieback should be as long as finished length from step 1 above, and as wide as ruffles that trim curtain, or slightly narrower.

4. Cut fabric bands. Aligning scissors with fabric grain (or with pattern, if off-grain), cut 2 strips that

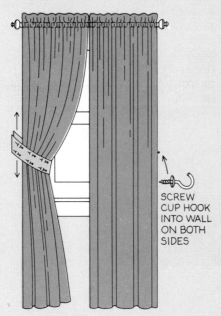

SCREW CUP HOOK INTO WALL ON BOTH SIDES

are each 1 inch longer than finished length of tieback and 3 inches wide.

5. Attach band to ruffle. On all sides of one band, turn raw edges under ½ inch and press. Fold band in half lengthwise, wrong sides together; press again. Pin a ruffle to band, having seam allowance of ruffle inside band, and aligning gathering stitching on ruffle with folded edges of band. Stitch close to folded edge of band.

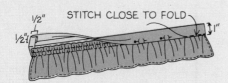

6. Hand-sew plastic rings to back of tieback, centered ¼ inch from each end.

Double-ruffle tiebacks

For a pair of tiebacks, you'll need fabric, four ½-inch-diameter plastic rings and two cup hooks. The fabric you use will affect the final appearance of these tiebacks. Crisp fabric will help ruffles stand up sprightly, while fabrics with less body may make ruffles that flop over along the upper edge of tieback.

1. Determine finished length of tieback as in step 1 of "Tailored tiebacks."

2. Screw cup hooks into wall as in step 2 of "Tailored tiebacks."

3. Make 2 double-edged ruffles, following directions on page 74. Ruffles for each tieback should be as long as finished length from step 1 above, and as wide as ruffles that trim curtain, or slightly narrower.

4. Cut fabric bands. Aligning scissors with fabric grain (or with pattern, if off-grain), cut 2 strips that are each 1 inch longer than the finished length of tieback and 1 inch wide.

5. Finish band edges. At each end of one band, turn raw edges under ½ inch and press. Fold band in half lengthwise, right sides together, and stitch ¼ inch from raw edges. Press seam allowance open.

6. Attach band to ruffle. Using a bodkin or safety pin, turn band right side out, positioning seamline at center back; press. Center band over gathering stitches and pin in place. Stitch close to long edges of band.

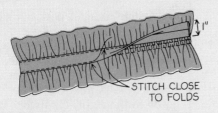

7. Hand-sew plastic rings to back of tieback, centered ¼ inch from each end.

Covered cord tiebacks

For a pair of tiebacks, you'll need fabric, plump cord—at least ½ inch in diameter—plus 2 cup hooks to attach the cord to the wall.

1. Determine finished length of tieback. Using length of string or strip of spare fabric, tie back panel at various positions until you are pleased with the way it drapes. Try different finishing touches—a simple loop, a loose knot, or a bow. To determine tieback length, measure length of string that gave desired effect.

2. Cut cords and fabric. Cut 2 lengths of cord, each twice the tieback length determined in step 1. Also, cut 2 strips of fabric, each 1 inch longer than the tieback length and 1 inch wider than the circumference of the cord.

3. Stitch casing. Starting at midpoint of one cord, wrap a strip of fabric around cord, right side in, as shown, making sure raw edges of fabric align. Using a zipper foot, stitch across fabric-covered cord ½ inch from cut edge of fabric. Raise presser foot, pivot work on needle, then sew down long edge of fabric, stitching close to cord (don't catch cord in seam).

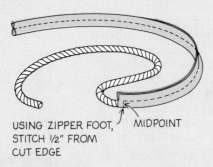

4. Turn casing. Holding end of encased cord, pull fabric tube right side out over other half of cord. At the cord's midpoint (where you started sewing), cut cord, slip a small amount of fabric back over cord's end, and blindstitch closed. At other end, slip back fabric, cut cord ½ inch short of fabric end, fold in raw edges of fabric, and blindstitch closed.

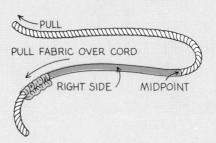

Special sack lining

Because they have rod pockets at both top and bottom, sash and hourglass styles are sack-lined slightly differently from the preceding method.

Hem allowances for one panel:

	Fabric	Lining
Bottom and top hems	As given for projects	none
Side hems	2 inches total	1 inch total

Note that for an hourglass curtain you'll need to add the stretch allowance explained at the beginning of that project. Begin with steps 1–5 of "Hourglass curtain," page 72; then proceed with step 2 below.

1. Measure for, buy, and prepare fabric and lining (see pages 36–47). Join widths if necessary, and press seams open. For sash curtains, measure the finished length on the lining panel and mark with pins; trim away ravel allowance.

2. Attach lining to face fabric. Pin lining to face fabric, right sides together, having side edges of both layers align, even though lining is narrower. Lining edge should be equidistant from face fabric edge at top and bottom. Stitch lining to face fabric at sides, making 1-inch seams.

LINING 1" NARROWER THAN FACE FABRIC

LINING CENTERED ON FACE FABRIC

1" SEAM

3. Turn panel right side out. When you turn panel, center lining so that an equal amount of face fabric shows on either side (just under ½ inch, depending on bulk of fabric). Position seam allowance toward center of panel; press. If you are making an hourglass curtain, return to page 73 and complete steps 7–13.

4. Trim top and bottom hems. Measure proper hem allowances on face fabric above and below remaining cut edges of lining. Trim away ravel allowance, leaving proper top and bottom hem allowances.

5. Turn top and bottom hems. Fold top edge of face fabric, wrong sides together, to meet edge of lining; press. Make second fold equal to the first, and press again. Stitch close to first fold, creating a rod pocket. Repeat at lower edge.

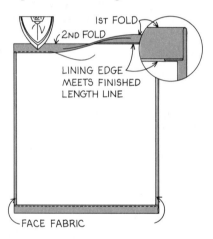

1ST FOLD

2ND FOLD

LINING EDGE MEETS FINISHED LENGTH LINE

FACE FABRIC

6. Follow steps 2–4 for "Rod pocket curtains with headings," page 57, if headings are desired.

Multiple shirred heading

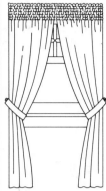

Fabric generously shirred in rows at the heading of a curtain forms tight little gathers that fall into sumptuous folds below (as shown in photograph on page 10). To truly show off such a style, you will need extra fullness—so multiply the finished width by 3 rather than the usual 2½ when calculating for yardage.

To shirr the heading, you'll need 3 strips of leftover lining selvages (pieced together as necessary) or ¼-inch-wide twill tape. The length of each strip should equal 3 times the finished width of the curtain, plus ½ yard. (For a two-panel treatment, cut tape in half.) To hang the curtains, you'll need enough drapery hooks to place one every 4 inches across each panel and at both ends of each panel.

For a two-panel treatment, just double the side hem allowance given below and repeat procedure for second panel. For a lined treatment, follow steps 1–9 for "Basic sack lining," page 66, omitting step 7; then proceed to step 2 below.

Hem allowances for one panel:

Lower hem	8 inches
Side hems	6 inches total
Top hem	7 inches

1. Follow steps 1–6 for "Basic café curtain," page 56, substituting the proper hem allowance where necessary.

2. Stitch casings. With left side of masking tape guide (see "A tape trick," page 48) positioned ¾ inch from sewing machine needle, stitch parallel to upper edge across panel. Move tape guide to the right, 1¼ inches from needle; move fabric and stitch a second row parallel to first. Make

4 more parallel rows of stitching, ½ inch apart (move tape guide ½ inch to the right for each one).

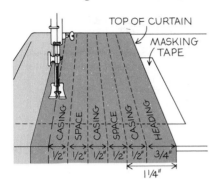

3. Insert tapes. The first casing begins at the first row of stitching from the top. Using bodkin or large safety pin, pull tape or left-over selvage through casing between back 2 layers of fabric, allowing at least 4 inches to extend at each end. Repeat for 2 remaining casings, skipping spaces between.

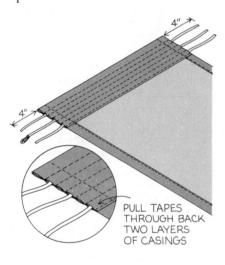

PULL TAPES THROUGH BACK TWO LAYERS OF CASINGS

4. Secure tapes. Stitch across one end of top hem, starting at upper

edge, 1½ inches in from side edge for unlined treatment or ½ inch in from side for lined treatment.

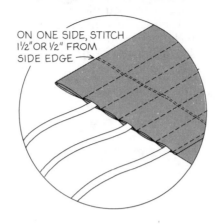

ON ONE SIDE, STITCH 1½" OR ½" FROM SIDE EDGE

5. Shirr heading. Lay panel wrong side up on padded work surface. Using T-pins or C-clamps, firmly secure stitched side of casing to padded surface or table edge. On opposite side, secure ends of tape or leftover selvages to padding with T-pins.

Working from stitched side, gather casings evenly over tapes or leftover selvages until panel width matches desired finished width; pin to secure gathering at unstitched end.

Stitch across open end of heading as in step 4. Clip tapes at each end of heading, leaving 1 inch extending; tuck ends inside casings.

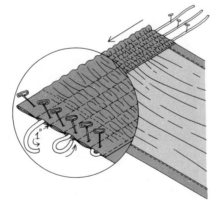

6. Insert drapery hooks. At each end of heading, 1½ inches from side edge, insert point of a 1-inch drapery hook 1¾ inches from top. Space remaining hooks between, about 4 inches apart.

Tab curtains

An imaginative alternative to rings, fabric tabs give café or full-length curtains a distinctly crisp, tailored look. You can make tabs to match or to complement the curtain fabric. If you choose the latter, consider going one step further and framing each panel with mitered trim to match the fabric tabs, as shown in the photograph on page 10.

When you measure the finished length for tab curtains (see page 37), adjust the starting point down below the rod 1½ to 2 inches. This space between the rod and the panel will determine the length of the tabs (see also "Starting point," page 37).

Allow ¼ yard of fabric for tabs. You can make at least 18 tabs from 54-inch-wide fabric—enough tabs for a curtain with a finished width up to 90 inches.

In calculating for fullness, you'll need to allow only 1½ to 2 times the finished width, rather than the usual 2½—which makes this style easier on the budget than most.

For a two-panel treatment, just double the side hem allowances given below and repeat procedure for second panel. For a lined treatment, follow steps 1–6 for "Basic sack lining," page 66, then proceed to step 2 below.

Hem allowances for one panel:

Lower hem	6 inches
Side hems	6 inches total
Top hem	2 inches

1. To make the curtain panel, follow steps 1–6 for a "Basic café curtain," page 56; do not stitch top hem as indicated in step 6.

2. Size of tabs. The finished width of each tab should be 1 inch, the cut width, 3 inches.

Determine the finished length of each tab by draping a strip of fabric or a shoelace over the rod, then measuring the distance from the adjusted starting point at the front, over the rod to the adjusted starting point at the back. Add 3 inches to this figure to get the cut length of each tab.

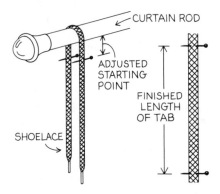

3. **How many spaces and tabs?** The visible space between the tabs, after the curtains are hung, will be 4 inches. The actual spacing of tabs across the panel will vary slightly, depending on the finished width of your treatment.

First, divide the finished width of the panel by 5 (width of one tab plus visible space between tabs). The result is the number of spaces your panel will have. With a tab at each end, the number of tabs will be one more than the number of spaces.

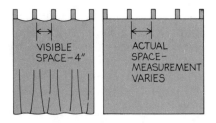

4. **Actual space between tabs.** Subtract the number of tabs from the flat panel width. Divide this result by the number of spaces to find the actual space between the fabric tabs.

5. **Make tabs.** For each tab, cut a strip of fabric on the straight grain to the cut length and width determined in step 2. Fold the strip in half lengthwise, right sides together, and stitch the length of the strip, ½ inch from

cut edges, leaving ends open. Trim seam allowance to ¼ inch. Turn tab right side out, and press so that the seam is at the center of tab. At ends, turn cut edges inside ½ inch; press and blindstitch closed. Fold tab in half crosswise.

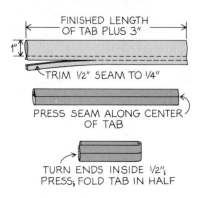

6. **Secure tabs.** For an unlined treatment, pin tabs on wrong side of panel as follows: Place each end tab flush with side edge, with lower edges of tab extending 1 inch below top edge of panel. Position remaining tabs between, separated by actual space determined in step 4. Machine-stitch each tab in place, ¼ inch from top edge.

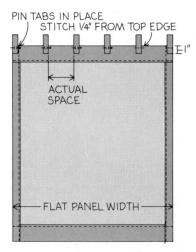

For a lined treatment, position tabs as above, but between face fabric and lining. Either machine-stitch across entire panel close to

fold of lining; or machine-stitch only across tabs, then blindstitch lining to face fabric by hand.

Hourglass curtain

Often seen on kitchen doors, this charming country classic evokes thoughts of homemade pies cooling on the counter and milk bottles rimmed with heavy cream.

In order to figure out the correct amount of fabric to buy, you'll need to add a special stretch allowance to accommodate the pinching in of fabric. For this, add 2 inches to the cut length for every 12 inches of finished length.

To make a lined treatment, first see "Special sack lining," page 70.

Stretch allowance for one panel:

Add 2 inches to cut length for every 12 inches of finished length.

Hem allowances for one panel:

Lower hem	Circumference of rod + 1½ inches (+ 2 times desired heading, if used)
Top hem	same as lower hem
Side hems	6 inches total

1. **Measure for, buy, and prepare fabric** (and lining, if used) as explained on pages 36–47. Join widths if necessary.

2. **Mark corners** of finished dimensions directly on padded work surface, using masking tape or pins.

3. **Determine side curves.** With synthetic tape measure or length of string, plot desired curves of hourglass shape on table from upper to lower corners (the two sides should be exactly the same). The narrowest part of the hourglass should be no less than ⅓ the width of window.

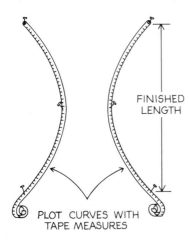

PLOT CURVES WITH TAPE MEASURES

FINISHED LENGTH

4. **Adjusted finished length.** The adjusted finished length is either the measurement read from the tape used to plot the side curve or the measurement of the length of the string.

5. **Mark fabric** (and lining, if used). On wrong side of face fabric, measure from one cut end and mark with pins the adjusted finished length measurement, plus hem allowances. Measure and mark on the lining (if used) only the finished length (lining has no upper or lower hem allowances).

Trim away ravel allowance and excess stretch allowance beyond pins; remove pins.

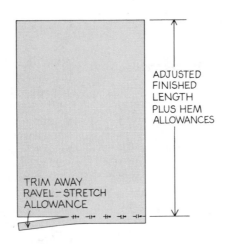

ADJUSTED FINISHED LENGTH PLUS HEM ALLOWANCES

TRIM AWAY RAVEL – STRETCH ALLOWANCE

For a lined treatment, turn now to "Special sack lining," page 70, and follow steps 2 and 3.

6. **Side hems.** Along each side of panel, fold and press a double 1½-inch hem. Stitch close to first fold.

1½"   1½"

7. **Fold panel in half lengthwise,** right sides together; press lightly. With pins, mark on the fold line each end of the *original* finished length measurement plus hem allowances. Check to be sure these pins are equidistant from ends of fabric.

8. **Mark curves and cut fabric** (and lining, if used). With very light pencil or chalk that you are sure will not show through fabric,

draw a curve at each end connecting pin at foldline to outer corners. Cut along these curves.

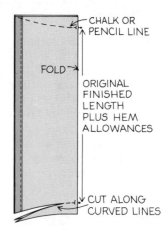

CHALK OR PENCIL LINE

FOLD

ORIGINAL FINISHED LENGTH PLUS HEM ALLOWANCES

CUT ALONG CURVED LINES

9. **To make rod pockets** without headings, first fold upper edge of fabric, wrong sides together, a distance equal to the proper hem allowance. Make a second fold equal to the first and press again. Stitch close to first fold. Repeat procedure for lower rod pocket.

To make rod pockets with headings, follow steps 2 and 3 under "Rod-pocket curtains with headings," page 57, for both upper and lower rod pockets.

10. **Insert sash rods** into rod pockets, gathering curtain evenly over rods. Mount curtain.

11. **Determine finished length of tieback.** With string or strip of scrap fabric, pull panel into hourglass shape at midpoint. Don't pull the curtain into less than ⅓ the width of the window. Add 2 inches for overlap; this is the finished length of the tieback.

12. **Cut tieback.** Add 1 inch to the finished length of tieback for seam allowances. For the width, choose either 2 or 3 inches, double that figure, then add 1 inch for seam allowances. Cut out a rectangle to these dimensions, aligning scissors with the grain or pattern.

13. **Make "Tailored tieback,"** following steps 5 and 6 on page 68. Wrap around curtain and pin or slipstitch in place.

Ruffling your curtain

Just as ruffles can soften the severity of clothing, they can soften the contours of curtains—adding a touch of romance at the same time.

Ruffles are fun, but they are time-consuming to make. You may be able to find them ready-made at a cost no greater than the cost of sewing your own.

If you prefer to design your own ruffled treatment, be sure to choose a fabric that gathers easily. Avoid dotted Swiss, because those charming little dots tend to catch the gathering thread.

Single or double?

A ruffle is simply a long strip of fabric gathered to frill along one or both sides.

Single-edged ruffles, gathered along one edge, frill on only one side. You can attach them to a curtain panel inconspicuously by using a French seam as explained on next page.

Double-edged ruffles are sometimes gathered down the center of the strip, creating two frills of equal depth. Or, if you prefer, you can run the gathering lines off-center, forming one ruffle and a narrower heading. (This is the kind of ruffle to use at the top of a rod-pocket curtain; the ruffle's heading should be the same width as the rod pocket.)

Measuring for ruffled curtains

Before measuring for yardage, you must decide which edges of the curtain panels you want to trim —typically, ruffles trim the lower hems and leading edges, and sometimes the headings as well. It will be helpful to make a diagram in your notebook at this point, showing the ruffled edges.

Next, you must decide upon a visible width for your ruffle and note its measurement on your diagram. In the case of a double ruffle, it is least confusing to consider the width of only the wider or outer frill as the ruffle's visible width.

First calculation

Your first calculation determines how much yardage you will need to make the curtains themselves. All you need to do is adjust the finished length and width measurements (see pages 36–38) for the treatment to account for the portions that will be taken up by ruffles.

If you will have ruffles along the lower hem, subtract the visible ruffle width from the finished length. To this figure, add 1 inch for a seam allowance for

attaching single-edged ruffles or ½ inch for attaching double-edged ruffles. Record the result as an adjusted finished length figure in your notebook. Ruffles along the heading will not affect your calculations for the panels themselves, as these ruffles hang down over the panel, rather than adding height.

If you will have ruffles along the leading edges, subtract twice their visible width from the finished width of the treatment. To this figure, add 2 inches for seam allowances for adding single-edged ruffles, or 1 inch for seam allowances for attaching double-edged ruffles. Again, record the result as your adjusted finished width.

Using the adjusted figures from your notebook, you can calculate total yardage for the panels alone, as explained on page 38, starting with "Total width."

Second calculation

To find how much additional yardage will be required for ruffles, follow the steps below. First you need to calculate the total width and the total length of the ruffle itself.

1. The total width of a single ruffle is simply its visible width measurement plus 1 inch (for hem and seam allowance).

If you plan to make double ruffles, first add the width of the narrower, or inside, frill to the visible width of the outer frill. Then add 1 inch for hems.

2. Divide the width of the fabric you plan to use by the total width of the ruffle. Disregard any fraction in the result. This whole number represents the number of strips you can cut from one width of fabric.

3. To find the total length of either type of ruffle, you use the finished width and length measurements for the *total* treatment (not the adjusted figures for panels-minus-ruffles). Account for the length of ruffles along the lower hem and/or heading with the finished width measurement; account for the length of those along the leading edges with the finished length measurement. Add these figures together as necessary to account for every ruffled edge in the treatment.

4. For fullness, multiply the result from step 3 by 2½ (for medium-weight fabric) or 3 (for delicate or sheer fabric). This result is the total length of the ruffles for the entire treatment.

5. To determine how much yardage you will need for ruffles, divide the total length of the ruffles by the result from step 2. Convert the resulting figure from inches to yards.

Final calculation

With total yardage figures for both curtain panels and ruffled trim, it is simply a matter of adding the two together to find how much fabric to buy. It would be wise to add an extra ½ yard as a margin for error in cutting out, seaming, or gathering the ruffle strips.

Making the ruffle

After cutting strips for ruffles, join them with narrow French seams (see page 49) to obtain the total length you need for each continuous ruffle you will make. After making the long strips, you are ready to hem and gather them.

Sewing the hem

In the case of a single ruffle, you fold, press, and stitch double ¼-inch hems on the two ends and one long side of the strip. If yours is a double ruffle, make the same kind of hem on all four edges of the strip.

Gathering ruffles

To gather the strip, set your sewing machine to its longest stitch. If your fabric can take it (practice first on a sample swatch), it might be wise to use heavy-duty thread.

For a single ruffle, run the first row of gathering stitches ½ inch from the raw edge. Stitch a second, parallel row halfway between the first row and the raw edge.

To gather a double ruffle, fold and press the strip lengthwise at the point that will divide the inside and outside frills. Open the strip again. Stitch each row of gathering stitches ⅛ inch from crease mark.

For either type of ruffle, stitch from one end toward the other, in segments about 45 inches long, leaving several inches of thread free at each end of the stitching. After stitching parallel rows, secure thread at one end of each segment to a pin on wrong side of fabric; insert pin as shown, wrapping thread in figure 8 fashion.

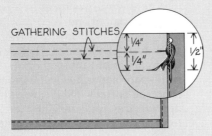

Holding the threads firmly on the opposite side of the segment, gently gather the strip over the thread until it becomes as short as its finished length measurement. With your fingernails or a straight pin, push the folds along until they are evenly spaced.

Attaching ruffle to panel

The proper way to attach a single ruffle to a panel is to use a French seam.

1. Align raw edge of ruffle with raw edge of panel, wrong sides together. Join with ½-inch seam. Trim seam allowance to ¼ inch. Press toward panel.

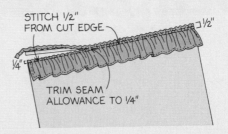

2. Fold ruffle over panel and seam allowance (right sides of panel and ruffle together); pin to hold.

3. Stitch ⅜ inch from fold, enclosing raw edges of ruffle and panel, as well as seamline. Press enclosed seam toward panel.

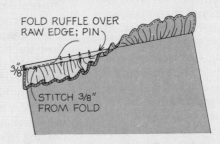

Before attaching a double ruffle to the leading edge or lower edge of a panel, fold, press, and stitch double ¼-inch hems on panel's raw edges.

Pin ruffle to panel so that wrong side of ruffle faces right side of panel; hem stitching on panel should be centered under gathering stitches of ruffle. Attach by stitching over hem stitching; remove gathering stitches.

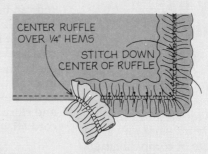

To attach double ruffle at top of panel, position gathering threads over stitching below rod pocket, then sew as above.

How to Make Draperies

While the dictionary makes no precise distinction between curtains and draperies, there is a commonly accepted one. Most people think of draperies as more luxurious and more formal than curtains—perhaps because draperies always have pleated headings and are often made of heavy fabric. Draperies usually traverse mechanically on a special rod but they can also hang as stationary panels.

Though you may find that making your own draperies involves more time and expense than making curtains or shades, your reward can be a very long-lasting and hard-working—as well as attractive—window covering. Draperies protect furnishings from fading and provide insulation, while adding a touch of luxury to your room. You may choose a single treatment, with the draperies suspended on their own, or a double treatment, which adds an underdrapery or curtain (usually made of sheer, translucent fabric to filter sunlight when the outer draperies are opened).

Drapery hardware and notions

Like curtain rods and brackets, hardware for draperies must be an early purchase. You'll need to know its dimensions and precisely where you'll install it before you can accurately measure for yardage. To be sure of compatibility, try to take a sample of the fabric you plan to use—or samples of several you are considering—when you shop for hardware.

Drapery rods

The best-known piece of hardware for draperies is the traverse rod, which enables you to open and close the panels by pulling a cord which moves little slides along a track, rather like operating a toy train. First developed early in this century, traverse rods are now available in a variety of styles ranging from the purely functional to the highly ornate. (If you plan to hang your panels as stationary draperies, choose one of the curtain rods listed on pages 51–52.) The following list should help you decide which style of traverse rod is right for your window.

Conventional two-way traverse rod. This plain-looking adjustable rod can be used on most windows for single treatments. The drapery hooks fit into tiny slides. The first two hooks on the leading edge of each panel fit into a "master slide" and the two master slides overlap at the center of the rod. You open and close the panels by pulling a cord attached to the master slides.

RETURN   MASTER SLIDE
END BRACKET   OVERLAP   PULLEY HOUSING

Conventional one-way traverse rod. This is similar to the preceding two-way rod, except that it moves only one panel in one direction and has only one return. This rod is often used over sliding glass doors—it can open from the right or from the left side.

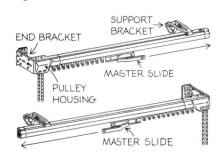

SUPPORT BRACKET
END BRACKET   MASTER SLIDE
PULLEY HOUSING
MASTER SLIDE

Where windows meet in a corner, use a pair of one-way rods that draw the panels from the corner to stack back at the sides, (below left). Or, in a situation where enough wall space separates the windows from the corner, install the rods to draw in the opposite direction—toward the corner (below right).

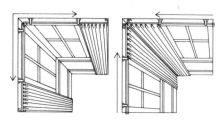

Over a bay window, you might place a one-way rod at each side, then use a two-way rod at the center, as shown.

Cut-to-measure rods are a common choice for bay, bow, or corner situations. These must be ordered for you by a drapery supplier.

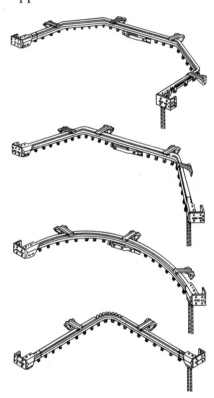

Decorative traverse rods. These rods are exposed whether the drapery is open or drawn closed. They are available only as two-way draws, but some types can be altered to move a single panel in one direction (check package to

see). They come with half-round ring-slides and with finials to attach to the ends.

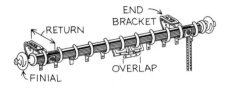

Traverse rod/flat curtain rod sets. You can buy several different types of these multiple-rod sets. For a double treatment with a curtain, buy a set with a decorative or conventional traverse rod on the outside and a flat curtain rod on the inside. If you want to

hang a valance over the drapery, use a set with the flat curtain rod on the outside, the traverse rod on the inside. (These traverse rods are two-way-draw only.)

Double two-way traverse rods. With this combination set, you can hang a double treatment; either one can be opened and closed.

Triple rod set. Use this combination of three rods if you plan a double drapery with a valance. The two inner rods are two-way

traverse types and the outside one is a flat valance rod.

Drapery brackets

Drapery rods come with two types of brackets—one type that holds the ends of the rod and another type that supports the rod at intervals along its length.

Both types of brackets can be adjusted to vary the distance the rod projects from the wall (called "rod return length"). For a single treatment, set the brackets to project 3½ inches. For a multiple treatment, adjust the brackets to their maximum projection.

End brackets, placed at the ends of a conventional two-way traverse rod, are hidden from view by the drapery panels, which curve back to the wall (below left). End brackets for decorative rods have a piece that fits under the round rod and attaches at the front with a decorative screw (below right). Special end brackets come with the multiple rod sets discussed earlier.

DECORATIVE SCREW

Support brackets ease some of the strain on long drapery rods. As a rule, you'll need one support bracket for every four feet of rod length—place one at the center of a four-foot-wide treatment. If your draperies are very wide or are made of heavy fabric, position a support bracket at the inside edge of each stackback area (when opened, the panels weigh most heavily on that part of the rod).

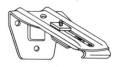

A one-way traverse rod is attached to the wall with a support bracket where the leading edge of the panel meets the end of the rod; at the other end, the rod attaches to an end bracket.

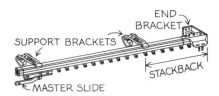

Hooks and weights

Small but significant, these two items play important roles in hanging draperies neatly.

Pin-on hooks. The most popular choice for attaching draperies to rods, pin-on hooks should be used at overlaps and returns, even if a different type of hook is used in between.

Three types of pin-on hooks are commonly used. A regular drapery hook (left) is designed to sit in the slide of a traverse rod without shifting under the weight of the fabric. Hooks with extra long shanks (center) are used to hold heavy, stiff headings upright. A valance hook (right) fits over a

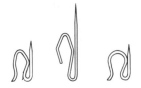

flat curtain rod, which is sometimes used in a double or stationary drapery treatment.

Slip-in hooks are easy to use because you just slip them inside the heading on either side of the pleat. However, they are not quite as stable as pin-on hooks.

Weights. To assure that panels will hang well, you can sew weights into the corners of the lower hem. The same types of weights are used for both draperies and curtains; they are discussed under "Weighting lower hems," page 64.

Hardware installation

More time-consuming than mounting a simple curtain rod, installing a drapery rod and adjusting it for smooth operation can be a demanding task. We've outlined the procedure below, but you should also find instructions in the package with your hardware.

Rod placement for draperies

Because traverse draperies are meant to be opened and closed, you'll need to extend the rod beyond the window at each side far enough to carry the entire stackback (see "Allowing for stackback," page 37).

To be sure that the back of the heading won't be visible from outside the window, you should position the rod at least 4 inches above the glass area.

Beyond these two considerations, placing a drapery rod involves the same decisions and

careful planning that go into placing a curtain rod. These are discussed under "Rod placement" for curtains, page 53.

Use the right fastener

To ensure a sturdy and secure installation, it is important to use fasteners that are suited to your type of wall or window frame and are strong enough to bear the weight of the rod and drapery (nails are not).

Wood screws are used to fasten brackets to solid wood—such as window casing or frame, paneling, or plywood—or to wall studs or ceiling joists. Although screws are packaged with drapery hardware, you can also use number 6 or 8 wood screws from the hardware store. To avoid splitting the wood be sure to make a pilot (or starter) hole with an awl or drill (the diameter of the drill bit should be slightly smaller than the diameter of the threaded portion of the screw).

Expansion bolts or toggle bolts are the proper fasteners for installation in wallboard or plaster. The expansion type (left) can be removed and reinstalled, while the toggle bolt (right) can be used only once. For either kind, you should first drill a clearance hole large enough to insert the bolt with its anchor mechanism folded. When the bolt is tightened, the anchor opens and grips the wall from behind.

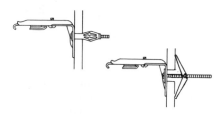

Masonry bolts are used for brick and concrete wall installations. You'll need a carbide drill bit to

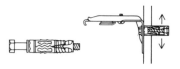

make a hole for the bolt. The hole should have the same diameter as the plastic plug on the bolt. When the bolt is screwed tight, the plug expands to grip the concrete securely.

Mounting a traverse rod

Before you embark on the adventure of installing and adjusting a traverse rod, a word of caution: Unless you are mechanically inclined, it can be a tricky business. Traverse rods with their accessories come packaged with instructions that are clear and adequate for the handyman or handywoman. If such is not a description of you, and if you feel at all confused as you read the manufacturer's directions, be sure to seek help from someone with experience.

Also bear in mind that before you can complete the installation, you need to know how many pleats your treatment will have (you'll need to adjust the number and placement of either slides or decorative rings to match the number of hooks). If you choose to purchase and mount the rod before making your drapery, first pick one of the two drapery styles presented (see pages 80-83) and, on paper, plot how many pleats you'll have in each panel.

As you follow the instructions that come with the packaged rod, you'll encounter these basic steps:
• First, you mount end brackets and any support brackets required. Be meticulous about doublechecking that the rod, when mounted, will be level and that marks on the wall for drilling are accurately placed.
• Next, you mount the rod. A conventional type simply slips into the end brackets. A decorative type is fussier to adjust—you need to arrange the rings (one for each pleat) in proper

position before you can tighten the brackets. For either type of rod, at this point you also adjust clips on any support brackets to fit snugly over the rod.
• Finally, you adjust the cord and mount the pulley. If yours is a conventional rod, this is the time to adjust the number of slides to match your number of hooks. One last word of warning: do not cut the cord until you've carefully checked that you allowed enough length to pull the panels completely closed.

Finishing touches

After the fussy and, at times, tedious business of sewing full-length draperies, the finishing touches of hanging and training them will make your victory sweeter. If you basted the lower hem during construction—a wise precaution, especially if you're using heavy fabric—finishing the hem will be your final step.

Hanging draperies

Invite a friend over to help you if you possibly can, because most draperies are heavy and awkward to handle. With the masters on the traverse rod in the closed position, you can begin hanging the panels. Start at the underlap master for a two-way-draw treatment, or at the single master for a one-way draw. Insert the first 2 hooks on the leading edge of the panel into the holes at the end of the master. Insert remaining hooks into slides and brackets. Hang the second panel the same way.

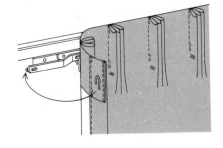

Training draperies

After being hung, draperies need to be "trained" so that their pleats and folds will cascade evenly from heading to floor. First, open the panels to the stackback position. Then, with your fingers, "comb" and smooth panels, pulling pleat folds forward and pushing back the folds in between. When all is even and smooth, gently tie the bundle in place with soft cord or fabric strips. If the cord tends to slip, carefully pin it in place. Leave the draperies tied this way for three days, then remove the cord—the folds should be set.

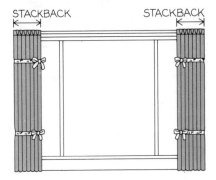

Basted hems

If you basted the lower hem during construction, you should let the drapery hang on the rod for at least a week before finishing the hem (see "Basting hems," page 50). At the end of that time the fabric may have stretched somewhat. Make any necessary adjustments in the hem; then take down the drapery and sew the hem permanently in place, either by hand or with machine blindstitching.

Pinch-pleated drapery

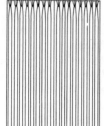

Follow these professional methods and achieve professional results— you'll spend considerably less money than you would for custom-made draperies.

When figuring total yardage for draperies (see pages 36–41), multiply by 2¼ for fullness instead of the usual 2½.

For each end of the panel and for every pleat, you'll need a pin-on drapery hook. You'll also need a strip of 4-inch wide stiffener (buckram or crinoline), cut 4½ inches shorter than the total width.

For a two-panel treatment, just double the side hem allowance given below and repeat procedure for second panel.

Unless made of sheer or open-weave fabric, draperies really should be lined. Besides adding body, lining will protect the face fabric from the sun and provide an extra layer of insulation.

For an unlined drapery, follow steps 1–4 for "Basic café curtains," page 56; then proceed with step 11 below. For attaching weights, see "Weighting lower hems," page 64.

Hem allowances for one panel:

	Fabric	Lining
Lower hem	8 inches	4 inches
Side hems	6 inches total	3 inches total
Top hem	8 inches	none

1. **Measure for, buy, and prepare fabric and lining** as described on pages 36–47. Join widths if necessary and press seams open.

2. **Lower hems.** Attach weights, if used, as explained under "Weighting lower hems," page 64. Then, with face fabric wrong side up, turn up 4 inches at lower edge; press. Fold up another 4 inches and press again. Blind-

stitch hem by hand, or—if you plan to let draperies hang before hemming (see "Basting hems," page 50)—machine-baste hem close to first fold.

Repeat for lower hem of lining, making each fold 2 inches deep (simply machine-stitch the lining hem closed, since it will be hidden).

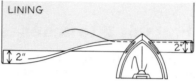

3. **Mark upper hem.** On the wrong side of the face fabric, measure up from the lower hem a distance equal to the finished length. Mark with pins placed every 4 inches across the panel.

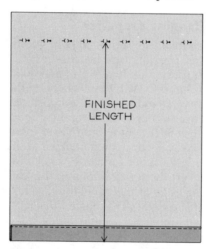

4. **Position lining and fabric.** With right sides together, lay lining fabric over face fabric so that lower edge of lining is 1 inch above that of face fabric. Align the first seams from leading edges of lining and face fabric.

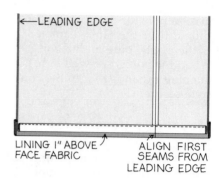

5. **Trim face fabric or lining** as necessary to make lining 3 inches narrower on each side.

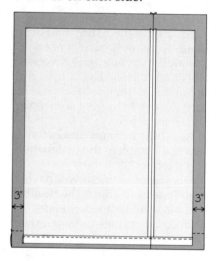

6. **Trim upper edges.** Trim away excess fabric along upper edge of lining so that lining edge meets pin-marked finished length line on face fabric. Then, on face fabric, measure and mark proper top hem allowance above finished length line, and trim away ravel allowance.

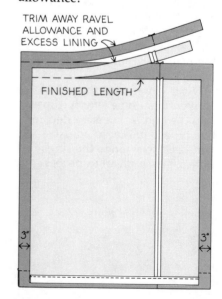

7. **Attach lining to leading edge.** Pin together lining and face fabric, right sides together, matching lining edge with leading edge of face fabric. Stitch a 1½-inch seam, starting at lower edge and stopping at the top edge of panel.

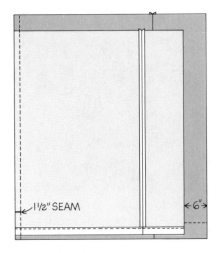

8. **Turn side hem.** Separate face fabric from lining, laying both, right sides down, flat against padded work surface. Press seam toward face fabric; fold seam

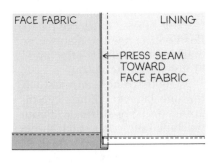

allowance and face fabric toward lining, wrong sides together; press.

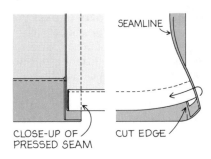

9. **Catch-stitch leading edge.** Fold back lining so that only one inch rests on face fabric. Insert needle with heavy-duty thread 10 inches from lower edge of panel, then take a catch-stitch in face fabric as shown, about 6 inches up. Take a second stitch, 6 inches above, in the lining. Stitches should be loose. Continue up the drapery panel, stopping 10 inches from the upper edge. Secure thread to lining fabric.

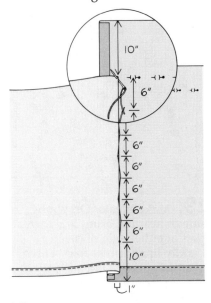

10. **Opposite side hem.** Unfold fabrics and return them to right-sides-together position, this time aligning remaining side edges of lining and face fabric (be careful not to pull out catch-stitching). Pin and stitch as in step 7. Turn panel right side out. Fold seam in toward center as you did in step 8 so an even amount of face fabric is showing at each side. Press.

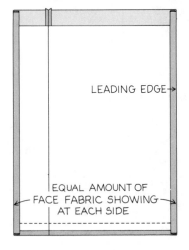

11. **Position stiffener.** Fold one end of stiffener under 1 inch; place fold ¼ inch from side of panel, aligning lower edge of stiffener with lining edge; pin in place.

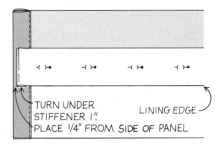

Smooth out remainder of stiffener to opposite side; fold under 1 inch at end of stiffener and position fold ¼ inch from edge of panel. Remove pins from finished length line.

12. **Turn top hem.** Remove pins from stiffener and fold the 4-inch allowance over it; press. Fold and press again; pin in place.

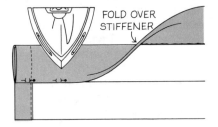

13. **Close sides of heading.** With stiffener in place, stitch sides of top hem closed, ⅛ inch from side edges, backstitching at each end. Stitch parallel to the first row, 1¼ inches from side edges, to hold stiffener in place.

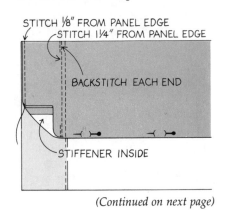

(Continued on next page)

Draperies **81**

14. **Subtract finished width** from width of flat panel for a single-panel treatment. For each panel of a two-panel treatment, subtract half the finished width from width of flat panel. Record result to use in step 16.

15. **Determine number of pleats and spaces.** Multiply the number of fabric widths used in each panel by 5 for full widths and by 2 for half-widths to find the number of pleats you can fit in the panel. The number of spaces between pleats will be one less than the number of pleats.

16. **Size of pleat.** Divide the result from step 14 by the number of pleats found in step 15. This figure is the fabric allowance for each pleat. Round off to nearest ¼ inch.

17. **Size of spaces.** For a single-panel treatment, subtract twice the rod return length from the finished width. For each panel of a two-panel treatment, subtract the rod return length plus 3½ inches from half the finished width.

Divide either result by the number of spaces between pleats (found in step 15); this figure is the fabric allowance for each space. Round it off to the nearest ¼ inch.

18. **Mark pleats and spaces.** At leading edge, measure in 3½ inches and mark with a pin. From this point measure and mark all pleats and spaces across heading, ending with a pleat. The portion of flat panel remaining should equal the rod return length. Because the calculations in steps 16 and 17 were rounded off to the

MEASURE IN 3½", OR RETURN LENGTH

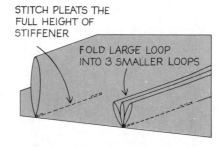

nearest ¼ inch, you may have to adjust pins slightly so that last pleat is positioned at the end of the rod. Also, if you have joined fabric widths to make up the panel, it's best to readjust pins so that seams fall close to the edges of pleats (making them practically invisible when the panel is hung). Be careful not to alter the size of the space when adjusting pins; make adjustments in pleats only.

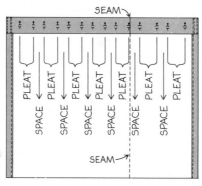

19. **Make pleats.** On wrong side of heading bring together pins at either side of pleat. Lightly finger-press fold. Stitch pleat from bottom of stiffener to top of panel at the point where pins meet (stitching line is parallel to fold). Backstitch at each end to hold pleat firmly in place.

Fold large loop into 3 smaller, even loops.

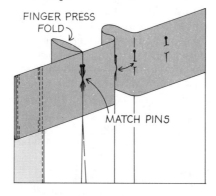

FINGER PRESS FOLD

MATCH PINS

STITCH PLEATS THE FULL HEIGHT OF STIFFENER

FOLD LARGE LOOP INTO 3 SMALLER LOOPS

Starting at the base of the pleat, stitch the loops in place through fabric and stiffener, as follows: Insert needle ¼ inch from fold of pleat and ¼ inch from bottom of stiffener. Stitch across pleat to vertical stitching.

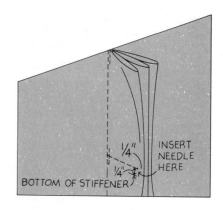

INSERT NEEDLE HERE

BOTTOM OF STIFFENER

Some professionals spray a small amount of silicone lubricant on the fabric and the needle to reduce friction and ease the passage of the needle through the fabric. (Look for silicone spray in hardware stores. Be sure to test a small sample on your fabric first.)

If you have a zigzag machine that can attach buttons, you can use this feature to secure pleats. Position the needle as above, set machine controls for attaching buttons, and tack pleat.

Some machines cannot stitch through 18 layers of fabric, 6 of lining, and 6 of stiffener. If your machine just won't stitch through the pleat, you'll need to tack it by hand. A sturdy needle and a thimble are necessary to push through the thickness.

After pleats are stitched, finger-press the folds above the tacking.

20. **Attach drapery hooks.** Pin a drapery hook to back of each pleat and at each end of panel so that it pierces stiffener, but not the face fabric. (See "Starting point," page 37, to determine where top edge of panel should be in relation to rod, and insert hooks accordingly.)

Box-pleated drapery

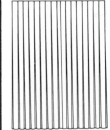

As a variation on the pleated theme, box pleats give draperies a tailored, rather geometric look. Their emphatic vertical lines appear to lengthen the treatment, which makes this style a prime candidate for wide windows (see photograph on page 12).

The fabric allowance for these pleats is 2 times the amount needed for spaces. When figuring total yardage (see page 39), first multiply the length of the rod by 3 for fullness and *then* add returns and overlap.

For each end of the panel and for every pleat, you'll need a pin-on drapery hook. You'll also need a strip of 4-inch-wide stiffener (buckram or crinoline), cut 4½ inches shorter than the total width.

For a two-panel treatment, just double the side hem allowances given below and repeat procedure for second panel.

Unless made of sheer or open-weave fabric, draperies really should be lined. Besides adding body, lining will protect the face fabric from the sun and provide an extra layer of insulation.

For an unlined drapery, follow steps 1–4 for "Basic café curtains," page 56; then steps 11–13 for "Pinch-pleated drapery," page 81; then proceed with step 2 below.

Hem allowances for one panel:

	Fabric	Lining
Bottom hem	8 inches	4 inches
Side hems	6 inches total	3 inches total
Top hem	8 inches	none

1. Follow steps 1–13 for "Pinch-pleated drapery," pages 80–81.

2. Determine pleats and spaces. For each panel of a two-panel treatment, divide half the rod length by 4 (the width of the visible portion of each pleat is 4 inches); for a single-panel treatment, divide the length of the rod by 4. Round off to lower whole number. This is the number of pleats and spaces in each panel.

3. Mark pleats and spaces. Starting at leading edge, measure in 3½ inches, plus 2 inches (half a space), and mark with a pin. From this point, measure and mark 8 inches for the first pleat. Then measure and mark 4 inches for the first full space. Continue measuring and marking all pleats and spaces across heading, ending with another half-space—2 inches—plus the rod return length. If you had to round off

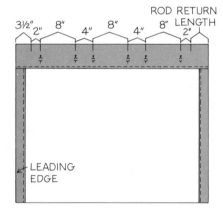

the number in step 2, you may have to adjust pins slightly so that last pleat is positioned at the end of the rod. Also, if you have joined fabric widths to make up the panel, it's best to readjust the pins so that any seam falls within a space or on the back of a pleat. Be careful not to alter the size of the space when adjusting pins; make adjustments in pleats only.

4. Make pleats. On wrong side of heading, bring together pins at either side of pleat. Where pins meet, stitch pleat from bottom of stiffener to top of panel (stitching

line is parallel to fold). Backstitch at each end of pleat.

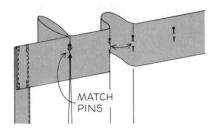

MATCH PINS

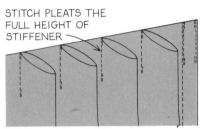

STITCH PLEATS THE FULL HEIGHT OF STIFFENER

Flatten large loop so that it lies against body of panel, centered over stitching.

At bottom of stiffener and top of panel, on either side of the flattened loop, tack pleats securely in place.

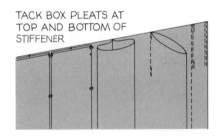

TACK BOX PLEATS AT TOP AND BOTTOM OF STIFFENER

5. Attach drapery hooks. Pin a drapery hook to back of each pleat and at each end of panel so that it pierces stiffener, but not face fabric. (See "Starting point," page 37, to determine where top edge of panel should be in relation to rod, and insert hooks accordingly.)

Cornices & valances

Topping off your window treatment with a cornice or valance not only adds an elegant finishing touch —it can also camouflage unsightly structural defects as well as frames, rods, and other hardware.

Are you unsure of the difference between a cornice and a valance? Both professionals and amateurs often use the terms interchangeably to describe any decorative treatment mounted across the top of the window. Strictly speaking, a cornice is a firm structure made of wood, buckram, or thick cardboard. It is painted, stained, or padded and upholstered, then mounted over the window treatment like an inverted window box. See pages 12, 15, 22, and 26 for photographed examples.

A valance, made entirely of fabric, is a softer and less permanent fixture that can be easily removed for cleaning. You can attach it to the mounting board of a Roman, Austrian, or balloon shade or simply shirr it, ruffle it, or tab it, and then hang it on a curtain rod. You'll find photographs of valances on pages 10, 15, 17, and 18.

Cornice and valance height

Before deciding on the top-to-bottom measurement of a cornice or valance, consider the height of your room and the length of your window covering. The total window treatment will be well proportioned if the height of the cornice or valance is about ⅛ the length of the window covering.

Also, be sure to consider tall people—you won't want the lower edge to fall at an annoying eye level.

A simple box cornice

You'll need:

Crosscut saw; saber saw or coping saw (optional); hammer; 4-penny finishing nails; 1-inch kiln-dried pine, fir, or other softwood (see steps 1 and 2 below for board measurements, adding at least 1 inch to board lengths as a margin for error); ⅜-inch interior fir plywood; white glue; paint brush; ¾-inch polyester padding (for a puffy, upholstered finish) or polyester foam batting (for a smoother, understuffed look); T-pins; staple gun; light to medium-weight fabric (see step 5 for amount); 1-inch angle irons and screws (or toggle or expansion bolts) for mounting.

1. Top board. Measure the width of the area you plan to cover (usually from bracket to bracket of the lower treatment), then add a 3 to 4-inch allowance at each end for hardware and fabric bulk. This should be the length of your top board. As a rule, the cornice should project about 2½ to 3 inches from the front of the rod, roller, or mounting board. This means that for a single drapery or curtain, the width of the

top board would be about 6 inches, while for bulky fabric or a double treatment, it would be 8 to 10 inches; over an outside-mounted decorative shade the projection should be 4 inches. After measuring and marking length and width on the piece of pine, cut the top board section. (Note: If sawing seems a chore, you can purchase your wood cut to measure.)

2. Legs. Cornice legs are as wide as the top board. Their length depends on the considerations mentioned under "Cornice and valance height" (generally, this will vary from 4 to 8 inches, less ¾ inch). Cut to your specifications, then glue and nail a cornice leg to the underside of the top board at each end.

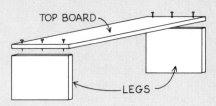

3. Face board. The face board is made from the plywood. Here you have the option of shaping the lower edge to make a decorative "apron." Scalloped or arched, select a design that will be perfectly symmetrical. To make a pattern, you'll need a sheet of paper as wide and as long as the outer dimensions of the box frame constructed in step 2. Fold the paper in half crosswise. Draw half of your design, starting at the fold and ending at the open edge of the paper; cut out the pattern through both thicknesses. Tape the paper to the plywood and follow the pattern with a coping saw or saber saw; sand edges.

For the standard, no-frills box cornice, cut the face board from plywood to fit the outer dimensions of the frame constructed in step 2.

Laying the frame on its back edges, glue and nail the face board to the front edges of top board and legs.

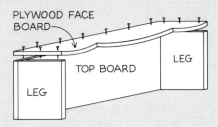

4. Upholstery. Cut the padding so that when it is completely wrapped around the cornice box, there will be at least one inch all around to tuck under. Dilute the white glue with water to the consistency of heavy cream; paint the box with enough glue to thoroughly wet the wood. Centering the padding on the upper edge of the face board, smooth it down the top board, tucking its edge to the underside of the top board. Stick T-pins through the padding and into the wood. Next, smooth the other edge of the padding taut over the face board and secure with T-pins to its underside. To reduce fullness, clip the padding where the legs and face board meet. Bring the clipped edges together and tuck under the legs, fastening with T-pins. After tucking and fastening remaining edge under each leg, allow glue to dry (about 20 minutes).

When glue is dry, miter inside corners and secure padding along the inside edges of the box with staples. Remove T-pins and trim off excess padding.

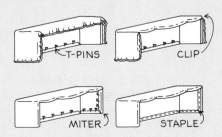

5. Fabric covering. Cut fabric 8 inches longer and 8 inches wider than the finished dimensions of the cornice box: (width of top board + height of face board) × (length of top board + twice the length of each leg). When glue is dry, center the box on the wrong side of the fabric, with the face board down.

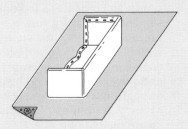

Tuck the fabric to the inside along the edge of each board, securing it with a staple at each corner. Then starting at the center of the top board edge facing you and working out to the corners, staple the fabric to the inside of the box every ¼ inch, smoothing fullness as you go. At either end of the top board you will need to cut (or tuck if your fabric is *very* thin) the bulk of accumulated fabric to provide a neat, taut appearance. To reduce fullness, pull fabric across the front ends and around the corners of the top board, make darts (their size depends on the fabric's bulk), turn to the underside, and staple. At the face board corners, follow the same procedure

of smoothing out fullness, cutting darts, and securing to the underside. Continue stapling until all fabric is secured.

6. Mounting. Anchor angle irons to wall above rod and window frame as shown. (See "Use the right fastener," page 78.) Mount and screw cornice box to angle irons.

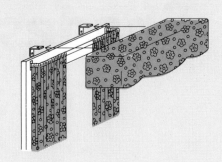

The versatile valance

Scalloped, shirred, plain, or pleated, soft fabric valances are the perky little miniskirts of the window treatment world. A valance is much simpler to construct than a cornice—you can easily make one to match or contrast with the lower treatment.

Where should you use a valance? In a very few situations, a valance would be inappropriate—for example, it would get in the way of casement windows that opened inward, and it might further dwarf the appearance of a room with a low ceiling. But in most situations, the possibilities for valances are virtually limitless.

Valances are charming toppings for all styles of curtains, for every variety of shade—even for formal draperies. The trick is to coordinate the valance style with that of its companion below.

To make a valance for a curtain, you simply duplicate in miniature the lower treatment, using the same top and side hem allowances but only half the lower hem allowance. Over draperies, mount a shortened version of the same drapery treatment.

Choose a suitable finished length for your valance following the considerations mentioned in "Cornice and valance height," then follow one of the curtain projects between pages 56 and 75 (remember to substitute half the lower hem allowance).

You can make an attractive valance for an inside-mounted Roman shade from a straight strip of fabric equal to the shade's finished width plus 8 inches (for double 2-inch side hems). Add 6 inches to the finished length measurement—4 inches for a double 2-inch lower hem and 2 inches for mounting allowance—and staple the valance to the mounting board for a neatly tailored finish (note the photograph on page 15).

How to Make Shades

Hard-working and functional, yet open to myriad decorating possibilities, fabric shades are understandably popular. Shades allow control of light and privacy, and they combine beautifully with many different styles of curtains and draperies.

Four style choices

In this section you'll find directions for making four different decorative fabric shades. We begin with the relatively tailored and simple-to-make roller shade. Next come Roman shades with their well-mannered folds, followed by the softly scalloped Austrian and billowing balloon styles.

Before you start...

Before starting a shade project, you should turn back to the beginning of this chapter and review the general guidelines for making window treatments. These three points are particularly important in successful shade-making.

• A padded work surface (see page 35 for directions for padding your own table) is especially helpful for measuring, pinning, and pressing large areas of fabric.

• For neat results, careful fabric selection is a must. Be sure that the fabric has a straight grain and that any pattern is aligned with the grain (also review "Adjustments for patterned fabric," starting on page 39). If the fabric is off-grain, your shade may not raise and lower smoothly; if the print is out of alignment with the grain, the finished effect may be visually disturbing. It's wise to buy fabric intended particularly for window coverings at drapery and upholstery suppliers. Or check the Yellow Pages to see if there is a window shade shop in your area —often such shops stock fabrics designed especially for shades.

• Finally, in making any window treatment, accurate measuring at every step is essential. The best tool for this is a steel tape measure.

Fabric suggestions

Your finished result will look best if you choose a fabric that conforms gracefully with the style of shade you make.

For a roller shade, look for a tightly woven fabric that won't fray easily—firm cottons and cotton blends (cotton/polyester and cotton/linen) are usually good choices. For sturdy canvas in sprightly colors, look at the selection available at shade and awning shops.

The note of distinction in a Roman shade is its series of military-crisp horizontal folds. For a neat, tailored-looking achievement, consider faille, cotton twill or duck, or a cotton/ linen blend. Try creasing the fabric with your hand—if this leaves a good impression, a shade made from the material is likely to fold reliably.

Traditionally, Austrian shades have been made of sheer or semi-sheer fabrics. Today, though, contemporary lightweight opaque fabrics—patterned or unpatterned —are joining the ranks as popular and practical choices. The important quality to look for in Austrian shade fabric, whether sheer or opaque, is its ability to drape softly. Nylon sheers, shantung, voile, and marquisette all carry this style gracefully.

True to its name, a balloon shade is airy, puffy, and rounded. Elegant, delicate, this style looks wonderful in a soft, supple fabric with sheen—such as chintz or antique satin. It should be opaque enough to conceal the back folds of the voluminous pleats that create the balloon effect.

Lining a Roman, Austrian, or balloon shade adds to its beauty and protects the face fabric (roller shades have special requirements; see "Stiffening a shade" on the next page). Choose drapery lining that hangs smoothly with the face fabric when you hold the two together.

Roller shades

Of the four shade styles in this section, roller shades require the least fabric and the least sewing. There are no seams or side hems and none of the pleats and gathers of Roman, Austrian, and balloon shades. Your task is to create a crisp, neat rectangle of fabric—the fabric you choose is really what gives this style of shade its pizzazz.

Stiffening a shade

Our roller shade projects, starting on page 88, offer you two ways to go in putting together your shade. Each calls for a different method of stiffening the shade.

Note: Although you can have a shade shop glue fabric to a plain manufactured roller shade, we do not recommend this method as a do-it-yourself project. The special adhesive used is tricky to apply—and it is rarely available through retail outlets. You will be better assured of success by following one of our methods for making a fabric roller shade from scratch.

As you decide which stiffener is for you, consider these points: Do you want the shade to screen out daylight completely—or can you accept some light filtering through? How will the shade appear from outside the house—or does this matter? Will the shade be unusually long?

Aerosol stiffener

Similar to laundry starch but producing much stiffer results, this product coats the fabric so that it becomes very crisp after it has dried and been pressed. Some light will filter through a shade stiffened this way because no extra "screen" is added to the basic fabric. Because it doesn't add a lot of bulk to the fabric, this product is probably your best choice for stiffening a shade that will be over 5 feet long.

You should be aware that some fabrics with special finishes will not absorb the stiffener effectively —and some fabric dyes may run. To be safe, test a sample of the fabric you plan to use to be sure it will take this method.

Spray-on shade stiffener is sold at stores that specialize in shades. Check by phone first to be sure of availability in your area.

Fusible webbing

Choose this stiffener if you want to line your shade with matching or contrasting fabric. A lined shade can create a striking decorative look from outside the house —but be sure any pattern on either layer of fabric doesn't show through on the opposite side (hold both to the light to check).

Fusible webbing comes only in narrow widths (18 inches is typical), which means you must overlap strips of it to cover the expanse of a shade. This webbing, also used in dressmaking, is sold in most fabric stores.

Hardware and fabric

There are also several ways to go when mounting a roller shade. You can place it inside the window opening (between the jambs) or outside, attached to either the frame or the wall. You can mount it so that the shade pulls down from front to back, exposing the shape of the roller to view (called "conventional roll")—or just the reverse, so the shape of the roller is hidden (called "reverse roll"). Because each option calls for a particular choice of hardware, you should decide which mounting and rolling position is best for

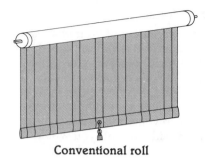

Conventional roll

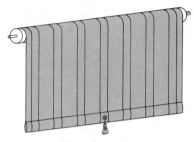

Reverse roll

your window before buying supplies. No matter which position you choose, here's the basic equipment you'll need for a roller shade: the roller itself, the proper mounting brackets, a slat to stiffen and weight the lower hem (comes with the roller), and a shade pull. If you are replacing an existing shade and will hang the new one the same way, there's no need to buy a new roller and brackets. Simply cut the new fabric to fit the roller you have.

Roller

The drawings on the next page show that a roller has two distinct ends—one with a pin and one with a blade. When you shorten a roller, the pin end is the end to cut off; the blade end contains the spring mechanism that makes the shade roll up.

Rollers are sold in many precut lengths, including 36, 45, 54, and 72 inches (the longer rollers are larger in diameter than the shorter ones). Don't feel bound to these sizes, though—it's a simple matter to cut through the soft wood of a roller. In fact, a good way to get a heftier roller is to buy a long roller and cut it down to the size you need (see "How to cut roller," page 88).

Brackets

The placement of your shade and the direction it will roll determine the type of brackets you will need. When mounted inside the window, one type of bracket serves both a conventional-roll and a reverse-roll shade. But for an outside mount, you would need one type of bracket for a conventional-roll shade and a different type for a reverse-roll shade.

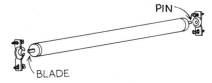

PIN

BLADE

Inside mounted, conventional roll

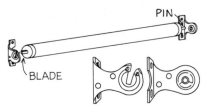

Inside brackets, conventional
or reverse roll

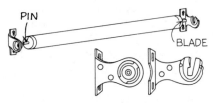

PIN

BLADE

Outside brackets, conventional roll

PIN

BLADE

Outside brackets, reverse roll

Installation

Once you have the correct type of brackets, it's best to install them before proceeding further. (For a shade that rolls smoothly, be sure to install the brackets so that the roller will be perfectly level.) Once the brackets are up, you can measure and cut your roller to fit.

Conventional roll. For a conventional-roll shade, the blade end of the roller should be on your left as you face the window. Mount the bracket with the slot on the left side and the bracket with round hole on the right (see drawing at left).

Reverse roll. For a reverse-roll shade, the blade end of the roller should be on the right as you face the window. Mount the bracket with the slot on the right side and the bracket with the round hole on the left (see drawing at left).

Inside mount. If your shade will hang inside the window jambs, you should mount the brackets about 1¼ inches down from the top of the window to allow room for the shade to roll smoothly. However, if your shade will be unusually long or thick, you may have to allow more room above the roller. In this case, mount your brackets about 2 inches down from the top of the window. Note: If your frame is very narrow and you mount the roller inside, a fine margin of glass may show on either side of the finished shade.

Outside mount. Place brackets for an outside-hung shade at least 1½ to 2 inches beyond the window opening on each side. This overlap will assure coverage of the window when the shade is drawn.

Measuring. Once the brackets are installed, measure the distance between the projections on the brackets to see how long your roller should be.

How to cut roller

Cut your roller from the pin end only. With a pair of pliers, remove the pin and the end cap. Cut the roller with an ordinary saw—be sure you don't cut through the spring (most rollers have a mark to indicate the end of the spring mechanism). Some shade shops will cut the roller for you, if you prefer. Replace the end cap and pound in the pin with a hammer.

Shade pulls

Standard pulls are designed to attach to the slat by screwing into it, slipping over it, or snapping onto it.

How much fabric?

The finished width of a roller shade is equal to the visible wood part of the roller after the roller has been cut to fit the brackets (see page 37). You'll need a cut length of fabric that is 3 inches wider than the finished width and 12 inches longer than the finished length.

Roller shade with spray-on stiffener

Special aerosol products for roller shades make stiffening the fabric a fast and easy task. Spray-on stiffener is not as widely available as fusible webbing, so you should check by phone with shade and drapery fabric shops in your area to be sure you can find it.

Also, this stiffening method is not suitable for all fabrics. Those with a stain-resistant finish may not absorb the spray—and occasionally the spray causes fabric dyes to run. Test the stiffener first on a sample of the fabric you plan to use.

1. **Measure for, buy, and prepare fabric** (see pages 36–47 and "How much fabric?" above). Square off cut ends of fabric (see "Cutting lengths," page 46).

2. **Trim sides.** Though you have already squared the fabric, you should double-check each corner to be sure it is a perfect right angle.

The finished width of the shade should be equal to the visible wood part of the roller. Center roller, perpendicular to sides of shade, across one end. After measuring carefully, mark trim lines as shown below. Cut with scissors along these lines, making long strokes and keeping shade perfectly flat.

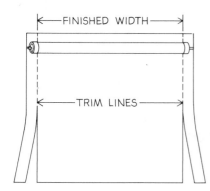

Note: It is important to use very sharp scissors and to make cuts as clean as possible.

3. **Sew slat pocket,** following step 6 of "Lined roller shades," page 90 (since fabric will not be stiff, you will need no helper).

4. **Spray shade.** Hang shade lengthwise, without folding it, in a well-ventilated place. An outdoor clothesline is ideal as long as the day is not windy.

Following manufacturer's directions, spray back of shade, being careful to cover every square inch. Let it dry, then spray front as you did the back. Allow the shade to dry completely before moving it.

5. **Touch up shade** with warm, dry iron to smooth out any dimple-like wrinkles which may result from spraying.

6. **Insert slat.** When pocket has cooled, cut slat to fit, and insert in pocket.

7. **Attach pull.** Attach pull to center of slat from either front or back of shade, as you prefer.

8. **Attach shade to roller.** Carefully align top edge of shade with guideline printed on roller. Be sure you have correct orientation of roller and shade for conventional or reverse roll (see drawings, page 88). Attach shade to roller with ¼-inch staples or flat-headed tacks.

9. **Optional precaution against fraying.** If your shade seems likely to fray along sides, (or if fraying occurs in future), you can "seal" edges with a white glue that dries clear and flexible. Put roller in brackets with shade fully extended. Put glue on a cotton swab and run swab along back edges, being careful to keep face of shade clean. Let glue dry completely before rolling shade.

Lined roller shade

The secret ingredient of a roller shade with a fabric lining is fusible webbing. Sold at fabric shops in narrow widths, this heat-sensitive material serves both to stiffen the shade and to bond together the face fabric and lining layers.

Check by phone to find a source for the widest possible webbing. Here's how to figure how much to buy: Divide the total width of your shade by the width of the webbing, rounding off the result to the next higher number if it contains a fraction. This will tell you how many strips of webbing you'll need across the width of the shade. Add 1 extra strip to allow for overlap unless (because of rounding off) you find you'll have enough excess webbing to allow 1 inch extra for each strip used. To calculate how much webbing you'll need, multiply the number of strips required by the cut length of the shade in inches, and divide by 36 to convert this figure to yards.

1. **Measure for, buy, and prepare face fabric and an equal amount of lining** (see pages 36–47 and "How much fabric?" on page 88). Calculate amount of webbing required as explained above, and buy webbing. Cut webbing into strips, each equal to the cut length figure.

2. **Square off cut ends** of face fabric·and lining as explained under "Cutting lengths," page 46. Press both carefully.

3. **Lay lining** wrong side up on padded work surface. Place lengthwise strips of webbing across width of lining, making ½-inch overlaps as shown below. Lay face fabric right side up over strips of webbing. Smooth it carefully until it is perfectly aligned with lining fabric.

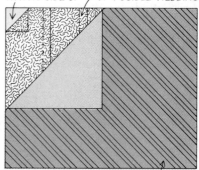

LINING FABRIC WRONG SIDE UP   OVERLAPPING STRIPS OF FUSIBLE WEBBING

SHADE FABRIC RIGHT SIDE UP

4. **Bond layers.** Using a damp press cloth and steam iron set for wool, press down in one spot at center of face fabric for about 15 seconds. Lift iron, move it to overlap first area, and press again for 15 seconds. Work from center out to edges in this fashion, dampening press cloth as needed.

After pressing right side, remove press cloth, turn shade over, and press lining side with steam—this time moving the iron

5. **Trim sides** of shade by following step 2 of "Roller shade with spray-on stiffener," at left.

The bottoms-up shade

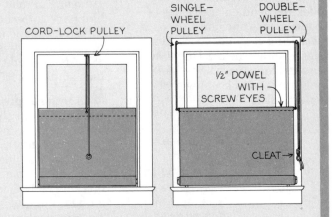

Delightfully upside down, this style of roller shade is mounted on the window sill (see the photograph on page 14). You raise it instead of lowering it. Serving the same practical function as a typical café curtain, it can provide privacy and exposure for daylight at the same time.

Because a bottoms-up shade conflicts with the law of gravity, to make it work you have to disengage the ratchet action of the roller and use a special mounting bracket. Many specialty shade shops sell hardware to simplify these alterations.

First, you'll need to buy a little sleeve that slips over the blade and locks the ratchet dogs. This releases the ratchet, leaving the spring tension intact. Because these sleeves come in several sizes, be sure to take your roller with you when you shop.

To keep the roller from being pulled out of its brackets, you'll need a special bracket for the blade end of the roller. You can use either a specialized bottoms-up bracket or an outside-mount bracket with two small holes above the notch for the blade. A small nail slipped through each hole in the bracket keeps the roller in place.

We offer three different ways to raise and lower a bottoms-up shade. You can employ one of two pulley systems—or you can operate the shade by hand, keeping it at various heights by slipping the ends of a metal rod (inserted in the slat pocket) into rod holders attached to the window frame.

The most flexible method is to use Venetian blind cord on a pulley system. You can either string a single cord up the center of your window to a cord-lock pulley, or run a cord along each side linked to two pulleys.

To attach a cord to the center of your slat,

first take your shade to a shade shop and have a rivet punched. Then tie the cord through the rivet and run it up to the pulley, mounted directly above and inside the window frame.

If you prefer to have the cords run up the sides of the window, use a ½-inch wooden dowel in place of a slat. Attach a screw eye into each end of the dowel and tie the cords through the eyes. Pick the more convenient side of the window for tying off the cords. Mount a double-wheel pulley at the upper corner of the window on that side and a single-wheel pulley on the opposite side. Run one cord up to the single-wheel pulley, across the top of the window to the double-wheel pulley, and then down to a tie-off cleat. Run the other cord through the double-wheel pulley, then down to the cleat.

If you are content to stop your shade at one, two, or three particular heights, a simple method is to use a ⅜-inch solid metal rod instead of a wooden slat. Attach rod holders to the window jambs at the desired heights to keep the shade in position. Both rod and holders are available at hardware stores.

6. Sew slat pocket. Because shade will be wide and quite stiff, try to have a helper hold and guide the shade as you stitch.

Turn up lower edge, lining sides together, making 1½-inch fold; stitch 1¼ inches from folded edge, using the longest straight stitch setting on your machine. Press pocket, following ironing directions in step 4.

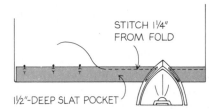

7. Finish shade by following steps 6 through 9 of "Roller shade with spray-on stiffener," page 89.

Roman shades

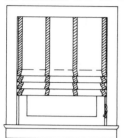

Though nearly as flat as a roller shade when unfurled, a Roman shade draws up into graceful crosswise folds. This accordian effect is accomplished by a simple system of rings and cords attached to the back of the shade.

Adaptable to many decors, a Roman shade can be finished with a simple hem, punctuated with crisp tucks, accented with contrasting trim, or dressed up with a decorative skirt (see "Decorating your shade," page 96).

Notions and hardware

Imagine what the backstage of a marionette theater must look like, and you'll have some idea of what goes on behind the scenes of a Roman shade.

To make your shade, you'll need some specialized notions from shops that carry shade and drapery supplies—as well as some general hardware store items. For rigging the shade, you'll need rings (about ½ inch in diameter) or Roman shade ring tape; Roman shade cord or lightweight traverse cord; screw eyes and a small awning cleat; and a ⅜-inch-diameter solid metal rod with a baked enamel finish (to prevent corrosion) that is 1 inch shorter than the width of your shade. To mount and hang the shade, you'll need a 1 by 2-inch board that is ¼ inch shorter than the finished width of the shade; staples or flatheaded

tacks for attaching the shade to the board; and screws to attach the board directly to the header above the window (for an inside-mounted shade) or right-angle brackets (with screws) for attaching the board outside the window frame.

Ring tape or rings?

For rigging a Roman shade, tiny rings are available either singly or attached at intervals to Roman shade tape. You should use tape if you are making an unlined shade; a lined shade looks best if made with individual rings.

Tape has some advantages—it strengthens the shade and saves you the job of measuring equal intervals between rings. However, individual rings cost less and allow you to select a vertical spacing to suit both the weight of your fabric and the depth of folds you desire. You will need to work out the placement of the tapes or rings for your particular project before you can know just how much tape or how many rings to buy.

Roman shade ring tape

Fabric

To determine how much fabric you'll need, start with the finished width and length (see pages 36–38) and add allowances for hems and mounting and for squaring ends. If you need to join fabric widths to reach the finished width, this will enter into your figuring.

Allowances

To your finished width, add 2 inches for two 1-inch side hems. To the finished length, add 2 inches for mounting the shade on the board, 1 inch to allow for raveling and squaring the ends, and (typically) 8 inches for a

double 4-inch bottom hem. The amount you allow for the bottom hem can vary, however, depending on the proportions of your shade. If you are making a short shade (up to 36 inches long), you may want only a double 3-inch hem; if your shade will be long (over 72 inches), you may want to make a double 6-inch hem.

On an outside-mounted shade, you may wish to add a decorative skirt—this will affect the cut length (see "Decorating your shade," page 96).

Joining widths of fabric

You might have to join fabric widths (or partial widths) in order to get the shade width you need. Refer to page 49 for a guide to symmetrical placement of fabric widths and for advice on matching pattern repeats when joining fabric. Also, when determining where to seam your fabric, keep in mind that you should have a row of rings behind each seam and that all rows of rings should be evenly spaced across the shade. (The success of a Roman shade depends in part on the shade's being a perfect rectangle, with square corners and parallel sides, so be sure that your seams are absolutely straight and parallel to the side edges.)

Because there is no fullness in the width of a Roman shade (the fit must be precise), you'll need to add a 1-inch allowance to your finished-width figure for each seam required.

Final figuring

Now that you know what allowances and adjustments to make, turn to "Total yardage for unpatterned fabric," or "Adjustments for patterned fabric," page 39, to figure your total fabric requirement.

Unlined Roman shade

Our first Roman shade project—the flat, unlined version—is the most basic style and the easiest to make. To rig this type of Roman shade, you use ring tape rather than individual rings. Read steps 7 and 9 below to work out how many rows of tape you will need. Buy ½ yard extra.

1. **Measure for, buy, and prepare fabric** (see pages 36–47 and "Fabric," page 91). Join widths, if necessary, with ½-inch seams and press seams open.

2. **Side hems.** With your fabric wrong side up, fold over each side edge 1 inch (wrong sides together) and press.

3. **Double bottom hem.** (Adjust these dimensions if you're making a wider or narrower hem.) Turn up bottom edge 8 inches (wrong sides together) and press. Unfold, turn up 4 inches, and press.

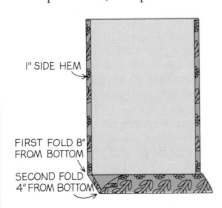

1" SIDE HEM

FIRST FOLD 8" FROM BOTTOM

SECOND FOLD 4" FROM BOTTOM

4. **Rod pocket.** Stitch across bottom hem 1½ inches from second fold, backstitching at each end. Fold fabric into double hem and press.

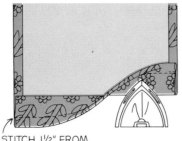

STITCH 1½" FROM SECOND FOLD

5. **Top edge of shade.** Overcast top edge with a wide zigzag stitch.

6. **Finished length.** On right side, measure up from bottom of hem and mark finished length at top of shade with pins. Fold top of shade down (wrong sides together) along pin-marked line and press. Remove pins.

7. **Side tapes.** On wrong side, starting at lower hem, pin Roman shade ring tape over side hems ½ inch in from the outside edges, as shown at right. Position tape so that bottom ring is at the top of the hem; cut tape 1½ inches below bottom ring. Cut upper end of tape even with top of shade, then determine if any rings should be removed. The space between the last ring and the finished-length crease should be more than half the distance between the rings. For example, if you are working with tape that has rings spaced 5 inches apart, your top ring should be at least 3 inches down from the crease. Cut off any extra rings.

8. **Sew on side tapes.** Using a zipper foot, stitch side tapes to fabric (they tend to stretch and pucker, so you may want to test your stitch tension first with a scrap of tape). Starting at the bottom ring (leaving the lower 1½ inches of tape loose), stitch along each edge of tape to top of shade.

9. **Remaining tapes.** On the wrong side of the shade between side tapes, mark the positions for additional rows of tape, evenly spaced about every 8 to 12 inches. If you have made seams to join fabric widths, trim the seam allowances to ¼ inch and position a row of tape over each one. Pin tapes as you did in step 7, making sure that the rings on all tapes align horizontally. Sew tapes as in step 8.

10. **Sew lower hem.** Tuck all loose tape ends inside hem. Sew across hem ¼ inch down from top fold.

11. **Insert rod.** Insert rod in pocket and whipstitch ends closed.

12. **Close bottom ends.** Slipstitch ends of bottom hem closed, being careful to not let stitching show on right side of shade.

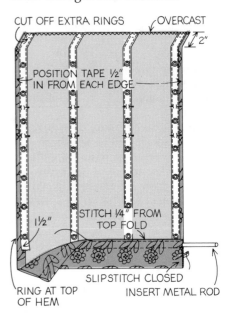

CUT OFF EXTRA RINGS

OVERCAST

2"

POSITION TAPE ½" IN FROM EACH EDGE

STITCH ¼" FROM TOP FOLD

1½"

RING AT TOP OF HEM

SLIPSTITCH CLOSED

INSERT METAL ROD

13. **Mounting board.** If part of the board will be visible once your shade is hung, you can paint it or cover it with cloth before mounting the shade.

14. **Staple shade to board.** Position shade right side up over 2-inch side of mounting board so that finished-length crease aligns with top front edge of board. Staple shade mounting allowance to top of board.

STAPLES

MOUNTING BOARD

FINISHED-LENGTH CREASE

15. **Insert screw eyes.** Turn shade and board over (wrong side up). Insert a screw eye in the bottom of the board above each row of rings (see below). Be sure to use screw eyes large enough to accommodate all the cords.

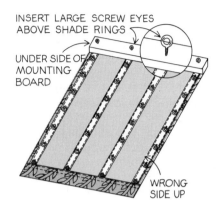

INSERT LARGE SCREW EYES ABOVE SHADE RINGS

UNDER SIDE OF MOUNTING BOARD

WRONG SIDE UP

16. **Cut cord.** Cut a separate length of cord for each row of rings. Each cord should be long enough to go up through a row of rings, across the top of the shade to the left, and half way down the side.

17. **Rig the rings.** With the shade still wrong side up, thread the cord through the left-hand row of rings first. Tie one end of the cord to the bottom ring. Thread cord up through all rings in the row, passing it from right to left through screw eye at top of row; let end of cord hang down left side of shade. Repeat this procedure for all rows of rings, each time passing cord through all screw eyes to the left (see below). When you finish, ends of all cords should be on left side of shade.

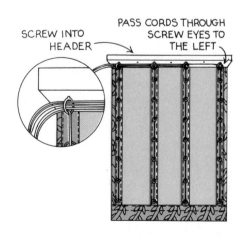

SCREW INTO HEADER

PASS CORDS THROUGH SCREW EYES TO THE LEFT

18. **Training and mounting.** Before hanging it at the window, it's a good idea to take time to "train" your Roman shade. To do this, lay the shade on a table, pull the cords to draw the shade up to the board, then tightly secure the cords. Straighten each horizontal fold and lightly crease the folds with your hands. When all folds are arranged, tie up the shade every 6 to 8 inches with strips of cloth. Keep your shade tied up for three or four days before proceeding. For an inside-mounted shade, screw the board directly into the header inside the top of the window (the narrow edge of the board faces out). For an outside-mounted shade, use right-angle brackets to attach the board (in the same position) to the face of the window frame or the wall.

19. **Tie off cords.** With the shade unfurled all the way, adjust the tension of the cords so that when they are pulled, the shade will draw up in even horizontal folds. When you are satisfied with the tension, lower the shade and knot the cords together just below the right-hand screw eye. Tie several more knots in the cords to allow you to stop the shade at different levels, then insert a cup hook or small awning cleat in the window frame to hook your knots under.

Lined Roman shade

Your lining should be the same length as the face fabric. The total width, after making any seams, should be 1 inch less than the width of the face fabric. If you have to seam together widths of lining, you should plan to have each lining seam align with a seam in the face fabric. Read steps 9 and 11 below to work out how many rings you will need.

1. **Measure for, buy, and prepare fabric and lining** (see pages 36–47 and "Fabric" on page 91). Join widths, if necessary, with ½-inch seams and press seams open.

2. **Bottom hem.** (Adjust these dimensions if you're making a wider or narrower hem.) With face fabric wrong side up, fold up bottom edge 8 inches (wrong sides together) and press. Unfold, turn up bottom edge 4 inches (wrong sides together) and press (as shown under step 3 of "Unlined Roman shade," page 92). Fold into double hem and press.

For hem in lining, repeat procedure for face fabric hem; however, finish step 3, below, before pressing double hem a second time.

3. **Rod pocket.** On lining, stitch all the way across 1½ inches from the 4-inch fold, backstitching at each end (see step 4 of "Unlined Roman shade," page 92). Fold lining into double hem and press.

4. **Join fabric and lining.** Place lining over face fabric, right sides together, raising lining so that its lower edge is ¼ inch above lower edge of face fabric. Pin lining to face fabric along side edges, aligning these edges even though lining is 1 inch narrower than face fabric. Make a ¾-inch seam along each side, stitching from bottom to top.

5. **Open rod pocket.** With lining side up, use sharp-pointed scissors to slit open one end of rod pocket. You should cut through only *one* layer of lining at least ¾ inch from stitching of one side seam. You will insert the rod later.

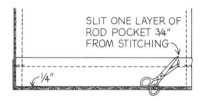

SLIT ONE LAYER OF ROD POCKET ¾" FROM STITCHING

¼"

6. **Sew hem.** Turn shade right side out and press flat, centering lining horizontally on face fabric. With the lining side up, stitch across full width of shade 3¾ inches above bottom of face fabric hem, backstitching at each end.

(Continued on next page)

7. **Top edge of shade.** Trim off excess lining at the top and overcast top edge with a wide zigzag stitch, joining lining to face fabric.

8. **Finished length.** On face fabric, measure up from the bottom of the hem and mark finished length with pins. Fold top of shade down (lining sides together) along pin-marked line and press. Remove pins.

9. **Mark vertical rows.** With lining side up, use tailor's chalk and a yardstick to mark vertical lines for rows of rings. Start your lines at the stitching at the top of the rod pocket and extend them to top of shade. The side rows should be 1 inch in from the side edges. Other vertical rows should be evenly spaced about every 8 to 12 inches. If you have made seams to join fabric widths, be sure to have a row of rings over each seam. Pin lining to face fabric along chalk lines; pins should be perpendicular to lines.

10. **Sew vertical rows.** To keep lining and face fabric in place and to add strength for sewing on rings, sew a straight seam over each chalk line (see drawing at right under step 12). Match the top thread on the machine to the lining and the bobbin thread to the face fabric. Remove pins.

11. **Ring spacing.** Mark with pins the positions of the rings. The bottom rings should be at the stitching at the top of the rod pocket. Spacing above the bottom rings depends on the depth of folds you want and the weight of your fabric. Typical spacing is 5 to 6 inches—but it could be as much as 8 inches for deep folds and heavy fabric. At the top, the space between the last ring and the finished-length crease should be more than half the distance between the rings. Be sure all ring marks align horizontally.

12. **Sew on rings.** Thread a needle with thread matching lining material (use a double strand of heavy-duty thread for firm

attachment with fewer stitches). Sew rings to lining only, carefully directing needle through lining and under row of vertical stitching.

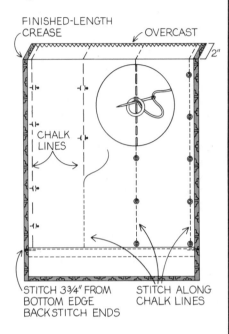

FINISHED-LENGTH CREASE

OVERCAST

CHALK LINES

STITCH 3¾" FROM BOTTOM EDGE BACKSTITCH ENDS

STITCH ALONG CHALK LINES

13. **Insert rod.** Fold hem up over shade (as if turning a cuff) and insert rod in pocket. Whipstitch rod pocket opening closed; turn hem down again.

14. Follow steps **13–19** for "Unlined Roman shade," pages 92–93, to mount shade.

Stitched Roman shade

The most tailored-looking Roman shade is this lined, stitched version. Stitching along the edge of each fold creates horizontal tucks when the shade is unfurled, and neat, accordion-style folds when the shade is drawn up.

Allowances for bottom hems, mounting, and side seams are the same as for other Roman shades: Allow 8 inches for a double 4-inch hem (adjust this if you're making a wider or narrower hem), 2 inches for mounting, 1 inch for raveling and squaring the ends,

and 2 inches for side seams. Lining material should be the same length as the face fabric but 1 inch narrower.

Because some of the fabric length (both face and lining) will be taken up in tucks, you must allow for this before you can calculate how much fabric you'll need. Note that slight variations in stitching each tuck can accumulate, causing the finished length to be an inch or so off. You may want to add an extra inch to your cut length to compensate; small adjustments can be made at the top of the shade after the folds have been stitched.

1. Determine the finished length.

2. Decide how deep you want the folds (typically 2½ to 4 inches). Divide the finished length by this figure. The result will tell you the total number of folds—front and back—your shade will have. Use the whole number and disregard any fractional part.

3. Decide how wide a tuck you want—how far away from the folded edge to run the stitching. Double this figure and multiply it by the number of folds to get the amount of extra fabric needed for tucks.

4. To the finished length, add the result of step 3 plus the allowances for hem and mounting, then add 1 inch to allow for raveling and for squaring ends. This gives you the cut length for both face fabric and lining.

Here's an example: Let's say you want a shade 60 inches long (finished length) with 3-inch-deep folds. Dividing 60 by 3, you find that you'll have 20 front and back folds. If you want stitching to run ¼ inch from each fold, then ½ inch of fabric will be taken up in each tuck. Because there are 20 folds, there will be 20 tucks. To figure how much extra fabric to allow for tucks, multiply the number of tucks (20) by the width of each tuck (½ inch). You'll need to add 10 inches (20 tucks × ½ inch) to your finished length, plus

10 inches for hem and mounting, plus 1 inch allowance for raveling and for squaring ends. Therefore, the cut length for both face and lining fabric will be 81 inches.

In these instructions we use the measurements given in the previous example. If you plan to have deeper or narrower folds or a different tuck width, substitute your figures at the appropriate places.

1. **For preparing basic shade,** follow steps 1 through 7 of "Lined Roman shade," pages 93–94.

2. **Finished length.** On face fabric, measure up from the bottom of the hem a distance equal to the finished length plus the extra allowance for tucks. Mark this distance across the shade with pins. Fold top of shade down, lining sides together, along pin-marked line, and press. Remove pins.

3. **Mark folds.** Working with the face fabric up, measure and mark folds, allowing for each tuck. Measure 3½ inches up from stitching at top of rod pocket and place a row of pins across the shade, pinning through face fabric and lining. Measure 7 inches up from pins and make another row of pins. Repeat every 7 inches ending with a row of pins 3 or more inches below the finished-length crease. Note that you will have one less **actual** fold than called for in your original calculations, but that the finished

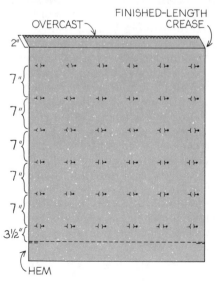

shade will nevertheless be the correct length.

4. **Make and press folds.** Turn the shade over so the lining side is up. Make a fold, with lining sides together, along the bottom row of pins, as shown below. Check to see that this and all succeeding fold lines are straight and perpendicular to the side edges. Remove pins and press fold.

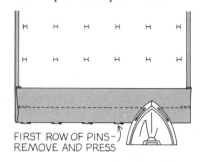

FIRST ROW OF PINS– REMOVE AND PRESS

Make the next fold (lining sides together) along the next row of pins; remove pins and press fold.

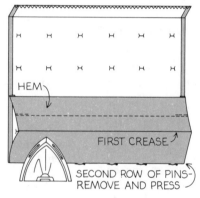

HEM

FIRST CREASE

SECOND ROW OF PINS– REMOVE AND PRESS

Then align the first folded edge with the second, with face fabric sides together, forming a back fold, and press. Accordian-pleat the rest of the shade the same way, bringing together two front folds to form one back fold.

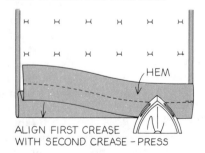

ALIGN FIRST CREASE WITH SECOND CREASE – PRESS

5. **Stitch folds.** Once all folds are pressed, stitch ¼ inch from the edge of each, to create tucks. On

both the top spool and the bobbin, use thread to match face fabric when stitching front folds and thread to match lining when stitching back folds.

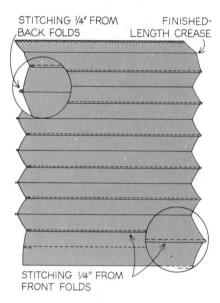

STITCHING ¼" FROM BACK FOLDS

FINISHED-LENGTH CREASE

STITCHING ¼" FROM FRONT FOLDS

6. **Mark for rings.** Working with the lining side up, mark the back tucks with pins for vertical rows of rings. The two outside rows should be 1 inch in from the sides; remaining rows should be evenly spaced about every 8 to 12 inches. If you have made seams, be sure to have a row of rings over each one.

7. **Sew on rings.** Using thread to match the lining, sew bottom rings at stitching at top of rod pocket. Sew all other rings through tucks on the back folds at pin marks.

8. **Insert rod.** Follow directions in step 13 of "Lined Roman shade," page 94.

9. **Follow steps 13–19 for "Unlined Roman shade," pages 92–93,** to mount shade.

Decorating your shade

The finishing touch of a decorative skirt or special trimming can give your roller or Roman shade precisely the flourish it needs. (The scallops and inverted pleats of Austrian and balloon shades make it difficult to add trim or skirts to these styles.)

The actual artistry is up to you—but here are a few tips and ideas to get you started.

Decorative skirt

When a shade has a skirt, the slat or rod usually falls at the bottom of the window sill, with the skirt hanging below. For this reason, skirts look best on outside-mounted shades.

Six inches is a common depth for a decorative skirt—but let the proportions of your shade guide you in deciding the most attractive depth. You can shape the skirt as you wish—experiment by drawing symmetrical designs, using curves or notches—perhaps even following the pattern of your fabric. The drawings below may give you further ideas.

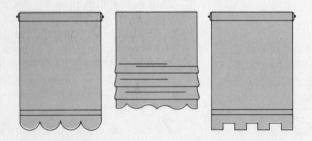

To make a symmetrical pattern, you'll need a strip of paper as long as the finished width of your shade and as wide as the depth you want for the skirt. Fold the paper in half, bringing the short sides together. Trace half of your design onto the folded paper; then cut out the design through both thicknesses.

Roller shade skirt

Add the depth of the skirt to the cut-length measurement for fabric and backing. Make your shade, following one of the projects on pages 88–90, up to the step of making the slat pocket. Then trace your pattern onto the bottom of the shade (wrong side) and cut the shade along the tracing.

Slat pocket. Place the slat pocket the distance of the skirt depth from the bottom of the shade.

If you used fusible webbing, sew the slat pocket this way: Fold the shade with wrong sides together, 3 inches above the top of the decorative skirt. Using a long machine stitch, sew across the width of the shade 1½ inches from the folded edge.

If you made your shade with iron-on shade backing, draw a line across the back of the shade 1½ inches above the top of the decorative skirt. Then draw a second line 3 inches above first line. Using a dry press cloth (or the paper liner off the backing), warm the area of the two lines with a dry iron. When the warmed shade is pliable, bring the two lines together. On the fabric side, press the fold down, forming the slat pocket. On the back of the shade, place a 2-inch-wide strip of iron-on backing, heat-sensitive side down, over the back of the slat pocket where the two lines meet. Bond the backing to the shade, using a dry press cloth and a dry iron set to the proper temperature for the fabric. Let the pocket cool completely before moving the shade.

Roman shade skirt

Just as you must plan in advance if you want to give a roller shade a skirt, you must make an early decision in the case of a Roman shade as well. To include a skirt, you will need extra yardage over that required for a plain, unadorned shade.

Unlined shade. To add a skirt to an unlined shade, you'll fold back the lower edge of the shade to form a facing. Your cut length will equal the finished length plus 1 inch for ravel allowance and squaring the ends, plus 2 inches for mounting allowance, plus 2 times depth of skirt.

To make facing, fold up lower edge of fabric, right sides together, a distance equal to the depth of the skirt. Trace design along fold. Then, starting ½ inch from top of facing, sew a 1-inch seam along the side edge, across the lower edge of the pattern, and up the other side, stopping ½ inch from top of facing. Cut out excess fabric, leaving ½-inch seam allowance; then clip curves. Turn right side out and press.

Referring to "Unlined Roman shade," page 92, follow steps 1 and 2, skip steps 3 and 4, and continue with steps 5 and 6, but in step 6, measure from the top of the skirt. Do step 7—except position the lowest ring at the top of the facing. In steps 8 and 9, start at the top of the facing (leaving the lowest 1½ inches of tape loose). Skip steps 10–12. Tuck all tape ends behind facing, turn facing edge under ½ inch, and sew across shade ¼ inch from fold. Cover rod with fabric and attach it to the shade as described in "Unlined balloon shade," page 103, steps 10 and 11.

Hang your shade following steps 13–19 under "Unlined Roman shade," beginning on page 92.

Lined shade. For a lined shade with a skirt, the lining should be 1 inch narrower than the face fabric, but the cut lengths of both lining and face fabric should be the same. The cut length will equal the finished length plus 1 inch for ravel allowance and squaring the ends, plus 2 inches for mounting allowance, plus depth of skirt, plus ¾ inch for seam allowance.

Place lining over face fabric, right sides together. Pin along side edges (align edges even though lining is 1 inch narrower). Sew from the top to the bottom making ¾-inch seams. With the fabric still wrong side out, smooth layers to center lining on face fabric. Trace skirt pattern on the lining, with the lowest point in the design ¾ inch above lower edge of lining fabric. Stitch over tracing, cut out excess fabric, leaving ½-inch seam allowance, then clip curves. Turn right side out and press.

Next, follow steps 7–9 of "Lined Roman shade," page 94. But in step 8, measure from the top of the skirt and in step 9, start lines at the top of the skirt. Continue with steps 10–12.

Cover rod with fabric as explained in "Unlined balloon shade," page 103, in step 10. Attach rod just below lowest rings by hand-stitching its case to shade lining. Mount your shade following steps 13–19 under "Unlined Roman shade," pages 92–93.

Decorative trim

Survey your choices before deciding how to trim your shade—you'll probably be surprised by the wide selection of styles, colors, and sizes of trims available. Let your imagination roam...consider rickrack, grosgrain or velvet ribbon, or bands of contrasting fabric. Note the banded white Roman shade in the photograph on page 15.

Trimming a roller shade

Use either a craft glue that dries clear and flexible or fusible webbing to attach trim to your shade—because sewing is likely to create wrinkles.

Confine trims to the bottom portion of your shade (the part that usually doesn't roll up), such as along the bottom edge.

Trimming a Roman shade

You can place flat trims—such as braid, ribbon, rickrack, or bands of fabric—virtually anywhere on a Roman shade. Sew the trim to your shade, being careful not to sew through the rod pocket.

For vertical rows, select a trim that's slightly wider than the ring tape (you may need to use a zipper foot). Stitch the trim to the right side of the shade, centering each row of trim over a row of rings. Starting just above the rod pocket, sew the trim to the top of the shade.

When adding a border of contrasting fabric, you should attach it before sewing the rod pocket. For an unlined shade, sew on the border after step 3 of "Unlined Roman shade," page 92, aligning lower edge of border with first crease made; then proceed with steps 4–19. For a lined shade, sew on the border before joining the lining and fabric. Make hem as in step 2 of "Lined Roman shade," page 93; then sew on border, remembering that 1¼ inches on each side of the fabric will be taken up in a side seam. After border is in place, proceed with steps 3–14.

The border will look neatest if you miter the corners as shown below. To do this, start with a single strip of ribbon, braid, or band of fabric (after turning under raw edges if necessary). Stitching about ⅛ inch from edge of trim, sew the outside edge down one side until you reach the bottom and are ready to turn a corner. Backstitch, raise the needle, and slide the fabric out from under the presser foot. Fold the trim back on itself as shown below. Finger press fold. Raise trim and hand-stitch a 45-degree diagonal seam along crease. If trim is bulky, cut away excess triangle underneath. Sew trim to bottom edge as you did to first side, mitering second corner like the first one. After sewing outer edge of trim, sew inner edge.

How to miter corners

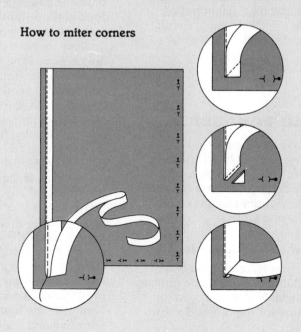

Austrian shades

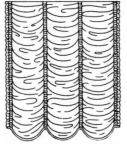

The Austrian shade is a kissing cousin of the Roman shade, but it is set apart by its shirring. This vertical shirring transforms the tailored folds of the Roman style into soft, draping scallops. The same marionette mechanism of rings and cords raises and lowers the Austrian shade.

Notions and hardware

The materials for making an Austrian shade are the same as those for making a Roman shade (see "Notions and hardware" and "Fabric," page 91), but substitute shirr tape (which comes with rings attached) for Roman shade tape. Shirr tape has two cords sewn to it that, when pulled, gather the shade fabric to create the scallops along the lower edge.

Plan your shade

Because an Austrian shade has fullness in both its width and length, you should plan your shade on paper so you can determine exact dimensions before purchasing fabric.

Finished width and length

Once you have decided where you'll mount your shade (inside or outside the frame), you can measure for the finished width and length (see "Measuring width and length," page 36).

While determining the width is straightforward, figuring the length of an Austrian shade requires some special consideration. It is difficult to precisely calculate how deep the scallops will be, so you should use for your planning a finished length equal to the distance from the top front edge of the mounting board to the metal rod at the bottom of the shirr tapes. The scallops, therefore, will fall below the finished length. For this reason, it is usually best to mount an Austrian shade outside the frame if you possibly can. (If you do choose to mount the shade inside the frame, you can, of course, adjust the finished length by taking up more fabric when you attach the shade to the board.)

Total width

Once you've determined the finished width, the next step is to decide on the number and size of the scallops. This calculation is based on your finished width minus 2 inches (one inch on each side of the finished shade will be taken up in a ruffle formed by the outside shirr tape).

Number and size of scallops. Each scallop should be 8 to 12 inches wide. Figuring how many scallops to make is easy if the area between the side tapes (finished width minus 2 inches) can be evenly divided by your chosen scallop width. For example, if your finished width were 56 inches and you wanted 9-inch-wide scallops, you would have six scallops (56 − 2 = 54; 54 ÷ 9 = 6).

However, if the computation using your shade size and scallop width leaves you with a fraction of a scallop, you'll need to make your scallops either slightly wider or narrower. Here's how to figure the size:

Start by assuming a scallop width of 10 inches (a good average size). Now take the figure representing your finished width minus 2 inches, and divide this by 10.

Suppose you had a finished width of 47 inches. You would divide 45 inches (47 − 2) by 10. Your result would indicate that you should have 4.5 scallops, each 10 inches wide. Since the number of scallops has to be a whole number, you'll need to round it off to either 4 scallops, each 11¼ inches wide (45 ÷ 4 = 11.25), or 5 scallops, each 9 inches wide (45 ÷ 5 = 9).

Scallop allowance. You'll need to allow 2 to 4 inches extra width for each scallop. The more width you allow, the deeper the scallops will be.

Side hems. Allow 1½ inches for each side hem—a total of 3 inches.

Number of fabric widths. Now calculate the total width so far and see how it compares with the width of the fabric you plan to use. Taking the figures from our first example, and figuring a 3-inch allowance for each scallop, this would be the sequence: Multiply the number of scallops by the scallop allowance (6 × 3 = 18). Add this to the finished-width figure (56), along with the 3-inch side hem allowance (56 + 18 + 3 = 77), and you find that you would have a total width *so far* of 77 inches. Therefore, if your fabric were 45 to 60 inches wide, you would need two widths of fabric.

Seam allowance. Add 1 inch to the total width for each seam needed to join fabric widths.

Joining widths

Join fabric widths only between scallops, not in the middle of a scallop. Drawing a picture of your shade will help you decide where seams should be (refer to page 49 for guidelines on symmetrical placement of fabric widths).

Here's how to map out the shade in our previous example: Draw a shade with six scallops. Each scallop requires 12 inches (9-inch-wide scallop + 3 inches for scallop allowance). On each side of the shade add 1 inch for a ruffle and 1½ inches for the side hem allowance (see diagram below).

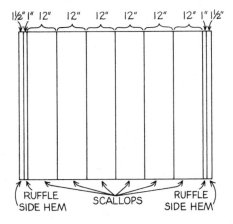

1½" 1" 12" 12" 12" 12" 12" 12" 1" 1½"

RUFFLE SIDE HEM   SCALLOPS   RUFFLE SIDE HEM

Now, counting left to right, you see that 48-inch-wide fabric would cover one side hem, one ruffle, and three scallops plus a fraction of another. But, because a seam should be made only between scallops, you must back up to an even three scallops. So, that portion of the shade would use a total of 39 inches (1½ inches for side hem + 1 inch for ruffle + 36 inches for three scallops + ½ inch for seam allowance) of a 48-inch width of fabric.

If you are working with patterned fabric, you should keep in mind that any side-to-side adjustment needed to match patterns horizontally may also limit the usable portion of a width of fabric. See "Adjustments for patterned fabric," page 39.

Cut length

Four factors in addition to the finished length make up the cut length: fullness, mounting allowance, bottom hem, and allowance for raveling and for squaring ends.

Fullness. Depending on the weight of your fabric, allow 2½ (for medium-weight) or 3 (for sheer) times the finished length for fullness.

Mounting allowance. Allow 2 inches at the top for mounting the shade onto the board.

Bottom hem. Allow 1 inch for a double ½-inch bottom hem.

Ravel allowance. Add 1 inch to allow for raveling and for squaring the ends.

In summary. Finished length multiplied by 2½ or 3 for fullness, plus 2 inches for mounting allowance, plus 1 inch for bottom hem, plus 1 inch allowance for raveling and for squaring ends equals the cut length.

How much fabric?

To find the total amount of fabric you'll need to make an Austrian shade, multiply the number of fabric widths times the cut length. For patterned fabrics, be sure to allow additional yardage for matching repeats (see "Adjustments for patterned fabric," page 39).

How much lining?

You will need to start with the same amount of lining as face fabric. Later, however, the lining will be trimmed so the width will be 3 inches less and the length will be 1 inch less than the face fabric.

If you must join lining widths, you should make seams at the same places where you seamed the face fabric. Then, when you assemble the shade, the seams will align, allowing the fabrics to drape well together. If your lining fabric is much narrower than your face fabric and you find that you can't always make seams so they align, you should at least make a lining seam at a point that will fall between two scallops.

How much shirr tape?

Each row of shirr tape will form a peak at the end of a scallop as the fabric is shirred. From the diagram in the left column, you can see that the number of rows of tape you'll need is one more than the number of scallops. The length of each row of tape should equal the fabric cut length plus 1 extra inch. Be sure to buy enough extra shirr tape to allow you to align rings horizontally.

Unlined Austrian shade

Once you have figured out on paper your finished shade size, scallop width, and seam placement, you are ready to proceed. Keep the drawing of your shade for handy reference.

1. **Measure for, buy, and prepare fabric** (see pages 36–47 and "Plan your shade," page 98).

2. **Seam fabric.** Making ½-inch seams, sew together all widths necessary for total width. Trim seam allowances to ¼ inch, then press open.

3. **Side hems.** Turn back 1½ inches on each side (wrong sides together) and press.

4. **Top edge of shade.** Overcast top edge with a wide zigzag stitch.

5. **Side tapes.** On the wrong side of the shade, place a strip of Austrian shirr tape over each pressed side hem, 1 inch in from the outer edge. Position tape so that the top of the first ring is 2 inches above the lower edge of the shade, then cut off the tape even with the lower edge of the shade (see below). Cut tape even with the top of the shade, and pin tape in place.

6. **Sew on side tapes.** Using a zipper foot, stitch side tapes to fabric. From top to bottom, stitch along each edge of tape; end with backstitching 2 inches above lower edge of shade (at top of lowest ring).

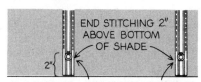

END STITCHING 2" ABOVE BOTTOM OF SHADE

2"

RINGS LINE UP WITH STITCHING

7. **Remaining tapes.** Pin remaining tapes in position according to your diagram (make sure rings align horizontally), and sew them in place as described in step 6. Keep seam allowances flat as you place tape over them.

(Continued on next page)

8. **Knot cords.** Pull out ends of shirring cords 1 inch down from the top of the shade (use a pin to separate threads of the loosely woven tape, then dig out each cord). Tie each pair of cords together securely in a square knot (see drawings below). Do the same at the lower edge, pulling out and tying the cords under bottom rings. Secure these lower cord ends to the tapes with overcast stitches.

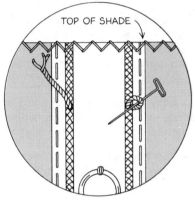

PULL OUT AND KNOT CORDS 1" BELOW TOP OF SHADE

PULL OUT AND KNOT CORDS 1½" ABOVE END OF TAPE

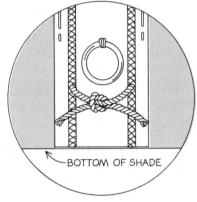

BOTTOM OF SHADE

9. **Rod loops.** Turn up raw edge of tape (right sides together) ½ inch, then turn up another ¾ inch to make rod loop. Stitch loop by hand just under ring, as shown in the next column, sewing through tape only, not shade fabric. Repeat for each tape end.

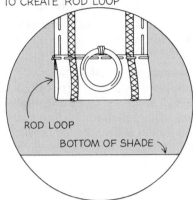

SLIPSTITCH CLOSED UNDER RING TO CREATE ROD LOOP

ROD LOOP

BOTTOM OF SHADE

10. **Bottom hem.** Make a double ½-inch hem by turning up raw edge ½ inch and then turning up ½ inch again. Pin in place, stitch across hem close to top fold, and press.

11. **Finished width.** Since the shade is now wider than the finished width (because of the allowance for scallops), you'll need to reduce the width by making tucks at the top of the shade next to the tapes. Make a small tuck at the inside edge of each side tape and at each edge of the remaining tapes. Start by making each tuck take up an amount of fabric equal to half the scallop allowance. Measure the width of the top of the shade and make any adjustments needed to make the top width equal to your finished width figure. Pin tucks in place on the right side of the shade.

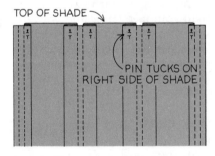

TOP OF SHADE

PIN TUCKS ON RIGHT SIDE OF SHADE

12. **Finished length.** With the shade wrong side up on a padded surface, use T-pins, centered between tapes, to fasten the bottom edge in a straight line. Pull the knotted cords at the top of the tapes, one tape at a time, to gather the shade until the length (from top to lower end of tapes)

equals the finished length plus 2 inches. Tie cords very tightly so shirring won't slip. Adjust gathers so the top 2 inches of the shade has no gathers and so the rings align horizontally.

13. **Cover rod.** To weight the bottom of your shade, use a ⅜-inch solid metal rod that is 1 inch shorter than the finished width. Cut a 2-inch-wide strip of fabric 1 inch longer than the rod. Fold fabric in half lengthwise, then stitch a ¼-inch seam across one end and along entire length. Turn cover inside out, insert rod, and slipstitch end closed.

14. **Insert rod.** Slip covered rod through loops at bottom of shade. Check to see that the shirr tapes are evenly spaced, then hand-stitch the rod loops to the rod cover to keep rod from shifting.

15. **Attach shade to mounting board.** Be sure all shirring cords are securely tied in square knots, then cut off excess cord extending beyond the top of the shade. Position shade right side up over 2-inch side of mounting board. Attach shade to board at top front edge, stapling over all cords and tucks (see below). Remove pins that were holding tucks. Fasten again at back of board, stapling twice over each cord to form an X.

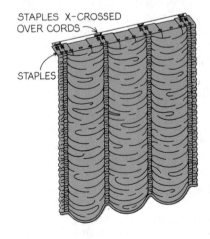

STAPLES X-CROSSED OVER CORDS

STAPLES

16. **Hang shade.** Follow steps 15 through 19—omitting the "training" part of step 18—under "Unlined Roman shade," pages 92–93.

Lined Austrian shade

The construction of a lined Austrian shade differs little from that of the unlined version.

1. **Measure for, buy, and prepare fabric and lining** (see pages 36–47 and "Plan your shade," page 98).

2. **Join widths.** Join widths of face fabric and lining, if necessary, making ½-inch seams. Press seams open.

3. **Cut lining to size.** Cut 1½ inches off each side and 1 inch off the bottom of the lining.

4. **Position lining.** Place lining on face fabric with wrong sides together, so that lining is centered horizontally on face fabric and their top edges are aligned. Pin lining in place, then remove pins as you proceed with construction.

5. **Side hems.** Turn each side of face fabric back over lining 1½ inches, and press.

6. **Follow steps 4–9** of "Unlined Austrian shade," pages 99–100.

7. **Bottom hem.** Make a double ½-inch bottom hem by turning up raw edge of face fabric ½ inch (wrong sides together), then turning up ½ inch again over lining, as shown below. Pin in place, stitch across hem close to top fold, and press.

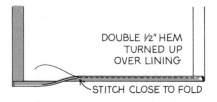

DOUBLE ½" HEM TURNED UP OVER LINING

STITCH CLOSE TO FOLD

8. **Finish with steps 11–16** of "Unlined Austrian shade" on the opposite page.

Balloon shades

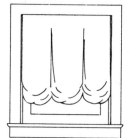

When a balloon shade is down, it has straight sides and a straight lower hem. The magic happens when you raise it— deep inverted pleats cause the shade to billow into puffs along the bottom edge.

Materials

The materials you'll need to make a balloon shade are the same as those needed to make a Roman shade (see "Notions and hardware" and "Fabric," page 91).

Plan your shade

In order to visualize your balloon shade and to know how much fabric you'll need, plan your project on paper first.

Finished width and length

A balloon shade can hang inside or outside the window frame. Decide which placement you prefer, then measure the finished width and length of your shade (see "Measuring width and length," page 36). This is straightforward, because a balloon shade is flat when unfurled—no scallops or puffs to contend with.

Total width

To determine the total width of the flat (unpleated) shade, first find out how many spaces between pleats you'll have, then calculate the size of the spaces.

Number of spaces. Using 10 inches as a rule of thumb for the width of each space, divide your finished width by 10 to get the number of spaces. If your answer contains a fraction, round it off to the next whole number. For example, if your finished width were 39 inches, dividing by 10 would give you 3.9—which would round off to four spaces.

Size of spaces. To find the exact width of spaces between pleats, divide the finished width by the number of spaces. If your finished width were 39 inches and you'll have four spaces, each space would be 9¾ inches wide.

Pleats. The fullness in the width of a balloon shade is provided by 3-inch-deep inverted pleats. The two pleats at the sides of the shade are single pleats; all other pleats are double. Note in the drawing below that there is one less double pleat than the number of spaces.

For each single pleat, add 6 inches to the finished width; add 12 inches for each double pleat.

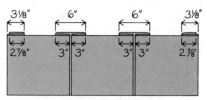

3⅛" 6" 6" 3⅛"
2⅞" 3" 3" 3" 3" 2⅞"

ALLOW 6" FOR EACH SINGLE PLEAT AND 12" FOR EACH DOUBLE PLEAT

Side hems. Allow 1 inch for each side hem for a total of 2 inches.

Number of fabric widths. Add up your flat panel width so far and divide it by the width of the fabric you plan to use. In our example, the total width so far would be the finished width of 39 inches plus 12 inches for two single side pleats plus 36 inches for three double pleats, plus 2 inches for side hems —which equals 89 inches. If your shade fabric were 48 inches wide, you'd need to divide 89 by 48. This would give you 1.8 widths, which must be rounded off to two widths of fabric (this allows plenty of extra fabric for a ½-inch seam to join the widths).

Seam placement

A seam in a balloon shade must fall within a pleat—either on a back fold or at the center back of the pleat. Drawing a picture of your shade (similar to the drawing on page 101), noting measurements, will help you determine where to put seams. From your drawing you can see that a width of fabric must cover *at least* the width of one side hem, plus one single pleat, plus the width of one space, plus a minimum of 3 inches into the first double pleat before you should make your first seam.

Amount of fabric

Once you know the number of fabric widths, you can figure out how much yardage you'll need: Multiply the cut length (finished length + double 1-inch hem + 2-inch mounting allowance + 1-inch ravel allowance) by the number of fabric widths.

If you are working with a patterned fabric, be sure to allow enough yardage to match the pattern repeat both horizontally and vertically (see pages 39–41).

How much lining?

If you are going to make a lined shade, you should start with the same amount of lining as face fabric. The lining will later be cut, however, to be 1 inch narrower and 2 inches shorter than the face fabric.

When you figure how much lining fabric you'll need, keep in mind that any seam joining lining widths should be placed where it will align with a seam in the face fabric.

Rings and ring tape

You will need a strip of Roman shade ring tape for each pleat (single or double) of an unlined shade. The length of each row of tape should be the same as the finished length of the shade. Buy enough extra ring tape to allow you to align rings horizontally.

If you will be using individual rings rather than ring tape, which is the usual method for a lined shade, buy enough rings to allow you to space them about 5 inches apart in vertical rows centered over the back of each pleat.

Unlined balloon shade

After working out your plan on paper, you are ready to create this delightful shade with its hemline cluster of fabric "balloons."

1. **Measure for, buy, and prepare fabric** (see pages 36–47 and "Plan your shade," page 101).

2. **Seam fabric.** Sew together all fabric widths, making ½-inch seams where they are charted on your drawing. (Allowances on seams that will be covered with ring tape should be trimmed to ¼ inch.) Press seams open.

3. **Side hems.** Turn back a 1-inch hem on each side (wrong sides together) and press.

4. **Mark tape placement.** On the wrong side of your fabric, using pins and a yardstick, mark the center of each double pleat.

5. **Sew on tape.** With your fabric wrong side up, place a strip of ring tape over each side hem, ½ inch in from the outer edge. Position each tape so the bottom ring is 3 inches up, and the end of the tape is 2 inches up from the bottom of the fabric. Pin tapes in place. Place all other strips of tape over pin marks made in step 4. Position tapes so that all rings align horizontally. Pin in place. Stitch along edges of tapes.

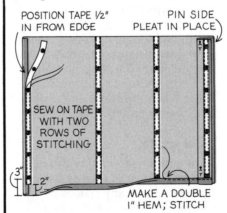

POSITION TAPE ½"
IN FROM EDGE

PIN SIDE
PLEAT IN PLACE

SEW ON TAPE WITH TWO ROWS OF STITCHING

3" 2"

MAKE A DOUBLE 1" HEM; STITCH

6. **Bottom hem.** Make a double 1-inch hem by turning up bottom edge 1 inch, wrong sides together;

press. Turn up hem again (over ends of tape), pin, then stitch close to upper edge; press (see drawing at left).

7. **Make pleats.** With your shade fabric wrong side up, make the single side pleats first. Fold over each side 6 inches, wrong sides together; then fold each side back over itself 2⅞ inches (see drawing at left). Pin pleats in place at top and bottom of shade.

To make the double inverted pleats across the shade, first fold the fabric with right sides together along a row of ring tape. Then, at the top and bottom of the shade, measure in 6 inches from the fold and mark there by pinning through both fabric layers. Next, flatten the 6-inch fold so the row of tape is centered over the pins, as shown below. Pin pleats in place at top and bottom edges, then remove marking pins.

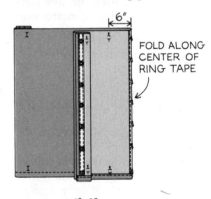

6"

FOLD ALONG CENTER OF RING TAPE

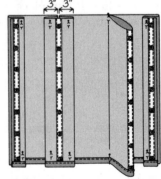

3" 3"

8. **Top edge of shade.** Overcast top edge (including pleats) with a wide zigzag stitch.

9. **Finished length.** Measuring from the bottom of the hem on the right side, mark finished length at top of shade with pins. Press pleats in place above this finished-length mark, then fold top of shade down along pin-marked line, with wrong sides together and pleats in place, and press just the crease. Don't press pleats in place below this line. Remove pins.

10. **Cover rod.** For the bottom of your shade, use a ⅜-inch solid metal rod that is 1 inch shorter than the finished width of your shade. Using a complementary lightweight material (such as drapery lining) or a remnant of your face fabric, cover the rod as follows: Cut a 2-inch-wide strip of fabric 1 inch longer than than rod. Fold fabric in half lengthwise, then stitch a ¼-inch seam across one end and along entire length. Turn inside out, insert rod, and slipstitch end closed.

11. **Attach rod.** Hand-sew rod cover to bottom hem just below first row of rings. At the back of each pleat, sew through rod cover and all layers of pleat except the face of your shade.

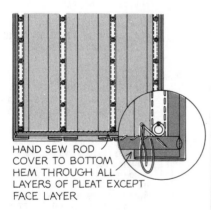

HAND SEW ROD COVER TO BOTTOM HEM THROUGH ALL LAYERS OF PLEAT EXCEPT FACE LAYER

12. **Staple shade to board.** Position shade right side up on mounting board so that finished-length crease is at the top front edge of the board. Fold shade mounting allowance over top of board and staple in place, stapling over each pleat and along back edge.

13. **Hang shade.** Follow directions given in steps 15 through 19 —omitting the "training" part of step 18—under "Unlined Roman shade," pages 92–93.

Lined balloon shade

When you make a lined balloon shade, you have a choice of using Roman shade ring tape or individual rings. The following method uses individual rings. Note that this project calls for tailor's chalk for marking rows of rings. Choose your chalk (or wax marker) carefully, and test it on your lining fabric to be sure it will not leave noticeable lines on the back of your shade.

If you want to make a lined shade and use ring tape, proceed with the following steps 1 through 5 and then turn to steps 5 through 13 under "Unlined balloon shade," starting on page 102.

1. **Measure for, buy, and prepare face fabric and lining** (see pages 36–47 and "Plan your shade," page 101).

2. **Seam fabric and lining.** Sew together all fabric widths, making ½-inch seams where they are charted on your drawing. Seam lining widths together in the same way. Press all seams open.

3. **Cut lining to size.** Cut ½ inch off each side and 2 inches off lower edge of lining.

4. **Join lining and fabric.** Place lining over face fabric (right sides together) so the two are aligned at the upper edge. Pin lining to face fabric along side edges (align side edges even though lining is 1 inch narrower than face fabric). Make a ¾-inch seam along each side. Turn material right side out and press.

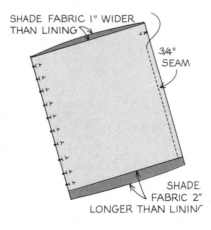

SHADE FABRIC 1" WIDER THAN LINING

¾" SEAM

SHADE FABRIC 2" LONGER THAN LINING

5. **Mark vertical rows.** With lining side up, use tailor's chalk and a yardstick to mark vertical lines for rows of rings. Start your lines at the bottom of the lining and go to the top of the shade. The side rows should be ½ inch from each edge. Each of the other vertical rows should represent the center of a pleat.

6. **Sew vertical rows.** To keep the lining and shade fabric in place and to add reinforcement for the rings, sew over chalk lines. Use a straight stitch, with top thread matching the lining and bobbin thread matching the shade fabric.

7. **Bottom hem.** Make a double 1-inch hem by turning up bottom edge of shade fabric 1 inch, wrong sides together; press. Then turn up hem 1 inch again (over lining), pin, and stitch across hem close to upper edge of fold. Press hem.

8. **Ring spacing.** With pins, mark each ring position. The bottom rings should be at the top of the hem. Space all other rings evenly, about 5 inches apart, with the top ring about 5 inches down from the top edge of the fabric. Be sure all rings will align horizontally.

9. **Sew on rings.** Thread needle with thread to match lining. Sew rings to lining only, carefully directing needle through lining and under row of vertical stitching, as shown in step 12 of "Lined Roman shade," page 94.

10. **Follow steps 7 through 13** under "Unlined balloon shade," page 102, noting that the metal rod should be covered with a strip of your lining material.

Index

Boldface numbers refer to color photographs.